LINDEMANN GROUP

Peter Schiessl

COREL PHOTO-PAINT 2021
&
PHOTO-PAINT ESSENTIALS 2021
HOME AND STUDENT 2021

Training Manual
with many Integrated Exercises

Icon arranged differently?
Window/Workspace/Standard
(not available for Essentials)

ISBN 979-8-482195-14-7
Print on demand since Sept. 22th 2021
Translated into English (US) by Peter Schiessl
V240925 / Lindemann Group
Publisher: Lindemann BHIT, Munich
Postal address: LE/Schiessl, Fortnerstr. 8, 80933 Munich, Germany
© MSc. (UAS) Peter Schiessl, Munich, Germany
Contact: E-Mail: post@kamiprint.de / Telefax: 0049 (0)89 99 95 46 83
www.lindemann-beer.com / www.kamiprint.de

All Rights Reserved.
Reproduction of individual pages, storage on data carriers, as well as any other use,
e.g., the use of the book or the exercises in a computer course,
if not every participant has acquired the book,
need the written permission of the author.
Place of jurisdiction is Munich.

This book has been prepared with the utmost care. However,
due to the variety of software and hardware, neither the publisher
nor the author can accept any liability for damage caused by errors
in the book or the programs described.

Product and prices are subject to change.

The names of the software and hardware are registered trademarks
of the respective manufacturers and were only mentioned for the
purpose of identifying the programs described and explained here.

This book was created from a full installation of CorelDraw 2023 in July 2023. Deviations from the descriptions and illustrations are possible due to a user-defined installation or changes due to other installed software or as a result of updates

Table of Contents

1. Preface

1.1 The Composition of this Book

By means of practical examples, all functions of PHOTO-PAINT are explained step by step:

- ◆ Firstly, the basic functions for painting. You need these basic functions when editing photos and creating your own designs.
  - ✋ Possible applications: Some advertising leaflets should look like hand-painted, and occasionally a line or a text should be added when processing photos.

- ◆ Then the possibilities to cut out objects (e.g., a human, ball, plane...) from a photograph.
  - ✋ This is a painstaking but everyday job for all those involved in professional image processing.
  - ✋ Such Objects can be inserted into other Images.
  - ✋ Possible with the extensive mask functions. Masks are frames for marking, what has been marked can be copied and pasted into other images or graphics.

- ◆ And finally, the numerous features PHOTO-PAINT functions for adjusting or distorting images with effects.
  - ✋ Good instance to correct the brightness of a scanned image or for effects like a perspective view, unrolled corners or the frog eye effect.

1.2 CorelDRAW and Corel Photo-Paint

Why CorelDRAW, why Corel PHOTO-PAINT? In Practice, both Programs are usually required:

- ◆ PHOTO-PAINT to edit photos with the computer: scanned photos, pictures from a digital camera, photos downloaded from the internet or from a photo DVD.

- ◆ Finished photos can then be combined with text and graphic elements in CorelDRAW to create a presentation slide, advertising leaflet, business card or poster, for example.

This division of labor results from a significant difference between vector graphics and pixel images, which will be explained in the next chapter.

1.3 Division of Labor in Practice

- ◆ Firstly, prepared Pictures or Photos in PHOTO-PAINT:
  - ↪ Scan or rework photos, cut out objects, variegate brightness, apply effects, etc.,
- ◆ then complete the presentation in CorelDRAW:
  - ↪ Load images, add text and your personal drawing elements = DtP.
- ◆ View advertising brochures: objects cut out of photos are always combined with other background and text.

What CorelDRAW is for	What Photo-Paint (Pixel) is for
Presentations	Scanning and post-editing images (e.g., correcting brightness, cutting away edges...).
Company logos	
Advertising leaflets	Edit photos (e.g., create an Image section).
Covers	Paint or edit images, Clip Arts in pixel formats.
Paint (detailed)	Painting (as if by hand, coarse, "simple children's pictures").
Drawings	Cut (crop) objects from photos, e.g., a person or an airplane. This object can be inserted into other photos or projects.
Business Cards, etc.	

Text processing should not be aimed at on a larger scale in any of these programs. Graphics programs are not designed for longer texts, so computer typesetting or word processing programs are better suited for this. Photos or clip art can also be inserted into these, e.g., photos prepared in the Photo-Paint in a club magazine.

1.4 What are Objects?

Take a look at your TV magazine or an advertising brochure. You will see that parts of a photo are placed in front of a completely different background, e.g., the image of a washing machine in front of a yellow contrast color or an actor without the background of the original photo.

To achieve this, the objects (human, fruit, washing machine, etc.) must be cut out of a photo, which is the classic application for Photo-Paint.

Since this is indispensable for professional work and also extremely interesting for private image processing, we will deal with this topic in detail. Since you cannot simply click and mark something in a photo, it's not so easy to see how it works without instructions.

To cut something out of a photo, first mark this area by creating a marker frame. It simply called Mask.

What is marked with a mask can be copied and pasted into the same image or any other file and is, therefore, an Object: objects are freely movable Picture parts.

1.5 Image Size and RAM Consumption

In photo projects, whether you are repainting or using an existing photo as a source material, the question of image size always arises, because, with high-resolution images, you can get huge files, but small photos, e.g., from the web, are too poor quality for professional projects.

- ♦ Small pictures, e.g., in photo size up to 10x15 cm for private projects:

  - ↳ At very good quality with 600 dpi scanned, the image is about 30 MB in size, compressed and stored in jpg format, which results in less than 3 MB.

- ♦ If, on the other hand, a photo is to be used as a background for a glossy title page in A4 format, the image file will be 50 to 200 MB in size at this required quality - per photo.

  - ↳ In addition, the professional sector usually stores uncompressed data to avoid any loss of quality.

  - RAM
  - ↳ That's why it makes sense to have as much RAM as possible for professional work with photos, otherwise, the computer becomes too slow because it has to be constantly moved to the hard disk.

  - ↳ For private image processing 4GB RAM (=working memory) should already be available, for professional at least 16GB and a fast SSD hard disk.

  - 64-bit
  - ↳ The 32-bit-Windows can manage a maximum of 3GB, so the 64-bit-Windows-Version or 64-bit Linux is also required.

The memory requirement of an image is determined by the number of points (=pixels of picture elements):

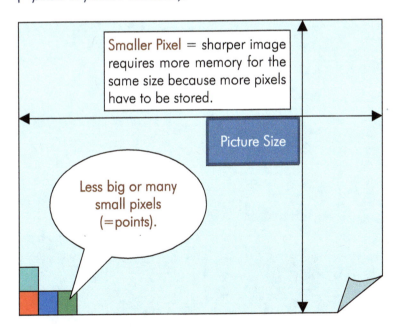

2. Vector or Pixels?

CorelDRAW is a vector drawing program, while PHOTO-PAINT saves the images as pixel graphics.

2.1 Vector Drawings

Drawing Elements (lines, circles, rectangles...) are saved as mathematical functions (vectors): line from point x1, y1 to x2, y2.

In the case of a line, the coordinates of the start and end point are noted, plus the line width, type and color.

- ♦ For this reason, any drawn element can be subsequently modified or moved.
- ♦ Even at enormous magnification, the lines always remain sharp.

Besides CorelDRAW, there are many other vector-oriented drawing programs, hence some different file extensions are used by these programs.

Of course, all CAD-Programs are the same

Vector programs (CAD = Computer Aided Design = computer-assisted drawing, programs for technical drawing).

2.2 Pixel Images

Similar to the screen or television, a photo is composed of many points on the computer.

- ♦ A very simple basic principle: for each of these Points, (=Pixels) the color is automatically stored.
  - ✎ Depending on the setting, your screen could consist of 1680 horizontal and 1050 vertical points (=Full-HD).
- ♦ This explains why the following problem exists with photo files: either large files or poor photo quality.
  - ✎ If pixel images are enlarged, the dots are clearly visible.
  - ✎ Instead of straight lines, stair steps can be seen as old dot-matrix printers.

Pixel Graphics Overview:

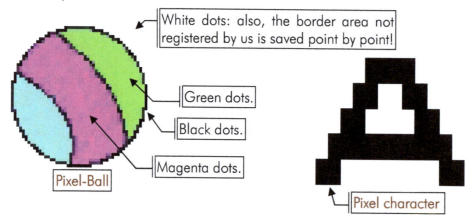

White dots: also, the border area not registered by us is saved point by point!

Green dots.

Black dots.

Magenta dots.

Pixel-Ball

Pixel character

Compressing:

- ◆ Even "empty" white areas are saved point by point. Here the file size can be reduced with compression.

  - ✆ The formula: from now on, 1000 x white points can be stored shorter than 1000 white points. This is why images with uniform areas (e.g., an even blue sky) can be compressed much more than totally colorful images.

- ◆ Disadvantages: with each loading or saving, the computer must calculate the compression as well as a small quality loss.

The best compression is the jpg file format. In PHOTO-PAINT, select Save as and specify jpg as the file type.

jpg

2.3 In Comparison

The differences between the two formats explain the advantages and disadvantages.

Advantages of vector graphics (CorelDRAW):

- ◆ Small files with sharp, precise lines and edges,

- ◆ Objects (e.g., rectangle, circle) can be modified as desired,

- ◆ Special effects are possible, e.g., Text Extrusion (expanding spatially).

What are Pixel Graphics (PHOTO-PAINT) used for?

- ◆ Pixel graphics are an inevitable evil because each scanner scans an image line by line, point by point, storing the color of each point. Also, a digital camera stores the image point by point, e.g., from 16 megapixels (=each photo consists of 16 million points).

Therefore, all photos in the computer are Pixel images.

- ◆ Another use case for a pixel program is Painting, as if using a brush and paint on a Screen. Some advertising graphics use this effect e.g., for pseudo children's pictures.

◆ Painting as if using brush and paint on Screen.

   ↳ is possible in PHOTO-PAINT: everything is painted over. The previous state can therefore not always be restored.

   ↳ Since it is difficult to paint with the mouse, a Drawing-tablet with a pressure-sensitive pen is recommended.

> However, the border to CorelDRAW runs smoothly and from version to version. More and more commands from PHOTO-PAINT are integrated into CorelDRAW and vice versa so that a program change becomes less necessary:

   ↳ in CorelDRAW, you can also edit photos with the commands from Photo-Paint. And in PHOTO-PAINT you can work with moveable and erasable objects.

Detailed for painting to drawing: a winter house with snow on the roof and a smoking chimney would make more sense in CorelDRAW because it can be corrected and changed at any time until everything deems fits because a window only needs to be drawn once and then copied as often as required.

2.4 The File-Types

2.4.1 Theory File Extension

There are many different graphics and photo programs. Each of these programs uses a specific file extension. Why?

◆ The File name can be up to 255 Characters long.

   ↳ Even spacebars and common special characters may be used, but no \ (backslash, this separates folders).

◆ The File Extension usually consists of three letters that are separated from the file name by a dot.

   ↳ Therefore, you should not use a dot in the File name.

   ↳ In addition, an icon is displayed for each file type and an explanatory text, for instance, "File type CorelDRAW graphic".

◆ As overview:

   ↳ Filename.cpt (cpt as File extension for Corel Photo-Paint).

File extensions

displays which program was used to create the file, so also what type of file it is, e.g., text document, photo, video or calculation.

2.4.2 Displaying File Extensions

However, it is practical to see the file extensions in order to distinguish photos from drawings in the file manager since Windows 95 file extensions are no longer displayed by default.

A quick guide on how to change the setting:

- ◆ In Windows Explorer click View, then Options,
- ◆ then disable the options
- ◆ from the index card view "Hide extensions for known file types" on the View tab:

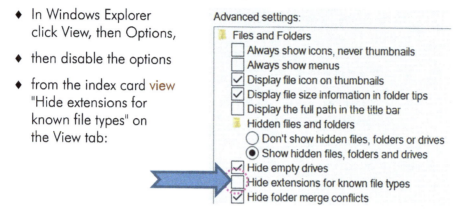

2.4.3 Convert File Types

If you want to open a Text in another word Processing Program, some formatting is usually lost. Fortunately, this conversion works perfectly for Photo Programs so that virtually any photo can be opened in Photo-Paint or exported to another format.

- ◆ If you have opened a photo, you can save it in another format with the command "File/Save as".
  - ✎ Select the desired type of file for a File type. With jpg, a menu appears, in which the compression level can be selected.
  - ✎ The default setting (10% Compression) reduces the file size by a factor of 10 with low quality-loss.

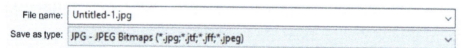

Masks or Objects can only be saved in PHOTO-PAINT format cpt. When converting to jpg, a message may appear that masks and objects are merged with the image. Masks are deleted and objects are permanently stored in the image.

- ◆ Not all Import and Export filters are loaded in the standard installation! If necessary, reinstall. To do this, restart Corel Setup and load the desired file formats.

- ◆ ClipArts and other vector files should not be opened in PHOTO-PAINT, as this would mean a loss of quality due to the conversion to pixel format!
  - ✎ PHOTO-PAINT is merely for photos (=Pixel images), CORELDRAW for Vector-drawings including used photos!

2.4.4 Examples of File Extension

Some knowledge of the file extensions is very useful to distinguish the file types:

File extensions for Vector Graphics (Drawings, Graphics)	
cdr	CorelDRAW-drawing.
ai	Adobe Illustrator-file.
eps	Encapsulated Postscript: a standard format for vector graphics from the Macintosh world.
dwg	AutoCAD-drawing (abbreviation of Drawing).
wmf	Windows Metafile: a format used by Microsoft, it is equally usable in Word as well as emf (enhanced metafile).

File extensions for Pixel-Graphics	
cpt	Corel PHOTO-PAINT - Image
pcx	In the past, many Clip-Arts were stored in this format. Formerly used extensively by Paintbrush.
bmp	Bitmap: format previously used by Windows.
tif	Target Image File: formerly the Standard-Format for scanned images.
gif	Graphic Image File: Good compression, but max. 256 colors, it is too low for photos but may be recommended for painted pixel graphics.
pcd	Kodak-Photo-CD-Pictures: correspondingly large files for excellent image quality. When copying to the hard disk, the image can be reduced to the desired quality.
jpg	Very good Compression, therefore highly recommended especially if a too large image is to be copied to a floppy disk and for the Internet or the photo collection.
png	Portable Network Graphics: Further development of gif and tif with compression without quality loss. Color reproduction however limited and compression not as good as jpg, so jpg is better for photos.
raw	Without compression: without loss of quality, mainly used by professionals.

On the Internet, transmission times are a problem, so photos should not be too long. Therefore, the jpg format is optimal for photos, drawn buttons are often created in gif format.

JPEG2000 (J2K, jp2) is a further advancement of the jpg format:

♦ In jpg, the image was split into 8x8 pixel groups which were calculated as zipped. With stronger compression from about 30%, these data become visible. With the new JPEG2000, however, the image is compressed as a complete Image. A higher compression with better quality can be achieved.

♦ More Color Information and more color fidelity on different devices, thanks to the sRGB color profile.

♦ Nevertheless, jp2 is rarely used because of more difficult settings and problematic for digital cameras with higher computing workload.

Part One

Painting in Photo-Paint like you would with a Pen or Brush on Paper

---

Most of these functions can be found on the left side in the Utility palette or at the top of the Property bar after the appropriate command has been selected in the utility palette.

> Don't forget a regular data backup! Photos in particular can represent an unimaginable ideal value, the loss of which would be a disaster. Backup copies online (cloud) in particular offer a high level of security.

2.5 Workspace

You can choose by Window/Workspace the workspace, Lite, Standard or Touch or Adobe Photoshop by Specialty:

- ◆ Depending on your choice, the icons and commands are arranged slightly differently.
- ◆ In the following we will use the working area "Default", the usual setting.
  - ✎ Lite is more reduced with as few symbols as possible, Touch is optimized for devices with touch-sensitive screens and Adobe Photoshop, of course, similar to the professional market leader program Photoshop from Adobe.

Icon arranged differently?
Window/Workspace/Standard
(not available for Essentials)

3. The Basic Functions

> Start Photo-Paint: double-click on the icon on the desktop or click on Corel Photo-Paint in the windows start menu in the CorelDraw-group.

Photo-Paint welcomes you with this welcome screen:

Corel PHOTO-PAINT
Essentials 2021 (6...

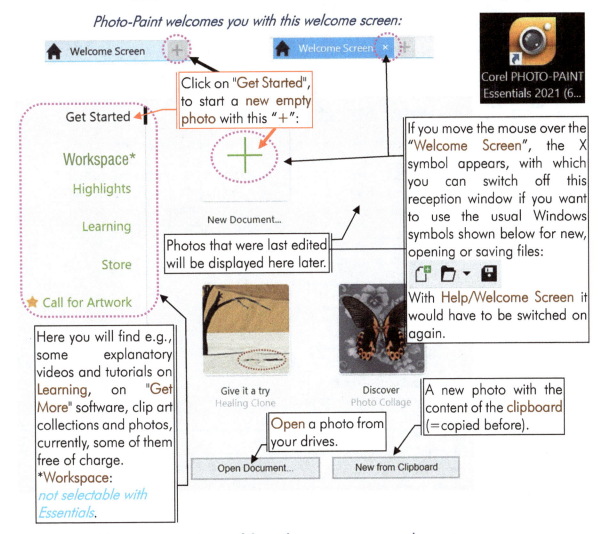

Click on "Get Started", to start a **new empty** photo with this "+":

Get Started

Workspace*

Highlights

Learning

Store

⭐ Call for Artwork

New Document...

Photos that were last edited will be displayed here later.

If you move the mouse over the "Welcome Screen", the X symbol appears, with which you can switch off this reception window if you want to use the usual Windows symbols shown below for new, opening or saving files:

With Help/Welcome Screen it would have to be switched on again.

Give it a try
Healing Clone

Discover
Photo Collage

Here you will find e.g., some explanatory videos and tutorials on Learning, on "Get More" software, clip art collections and photos, currently, some of them free of charge.
*Workspace:
not selectable with Essentials.

Open a photo from your drives.

A new photo with the content of the clipboard (=copied before).

Open Document...   New from Clipboard

You can use the icons of the welcome screen or usual icons to open, save:

> Select a **new Image** in one of the ways described above.

> ☝ Without the Welcome Screen above, you can do this like in any other program with the symbols in the top left (New / Open / Save).

> In the **window that appears** for the preselection, e.g., the drawing size, first switch to landscape format and the unit mm or inch, as you prefer, further information on the **resolution** follows on the next page.

3.1 New Image, First Painting

We'll start practically in a moment by drawing some rectangles.

➢ Select the setting 1024x768 pixels (=dots) for size in landscape, 150 dpi and RGB/24 Bit color modus, enough for this first training drawing.

➢ Select the rectangle tool shown and draw a Rectangle. Note: the dashed rectangle symbol at the top is for selected frames, use the symbol shown on the right.

➢ Select different colors from the color palette on the right, the following applies: left mouse button selects the fill color, clicking with the right mouse button selects a line color.

✍ You don't see the line color yet, because lines are switched off by default.

➢ Therefore, increase the line thickness at the top of the property bar and draw some more rectangles with different line and fill colors.

3.2 The Photo-Paint Structure

Now you have a picture and we can deal with the installation of Photo-Paint.

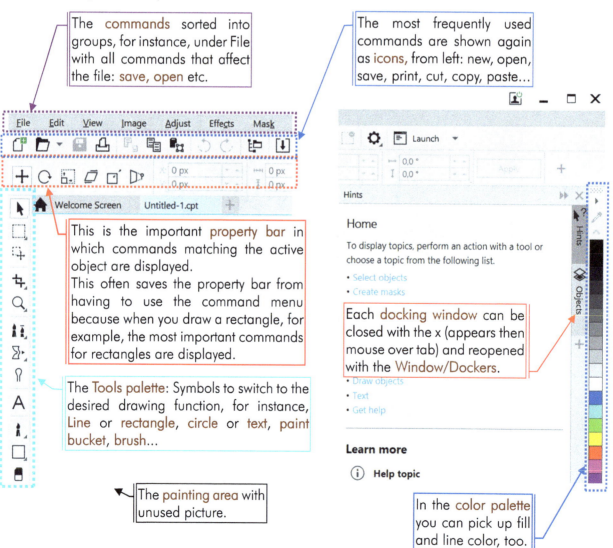

The commands sorted into groups, for instance, under File with all commands that affect the file: save, open etc.

The most frequently used commands are shown again as icons, from left: new, open, save, print, cut, copy, paste...

This is the important property bar in which commands matching the active object are displayed.
This often saves the property bar from having to use the command menu because when you draw a rectangle, for example, the most important commands for rectangles are displayed.

The Tools palette: Symbols to switch to the desired drawing function, for instance, Line or rectangle, circle or text, paint bucket, brush...

Each docking window can be closed with the x (appears then mouse over tab) and reopened with the Window/Dockers.

The painting area with unused picture.

In the color palette you can pick up fill and line color, too.

> ➤ Close the docker windows on the right by clicking on the respective X symbol in the tab. Then enlarge the image to the maximum.

[F4] = fit

>> ↪ You can reopen anytime by Window/Dockers if you need one of them.

Now it is saved, then the drawing tools are introduced one after the other and the use of the colors is practiced.

3.3 Save

Save is only possible after something has been drawn or changed.

> ➤ Open the Save menu by clicking on the Save icon in the upper left because a computer crash is never excluded!

Where to save? Please avoid putting your hard drive anywhere!

New folder

> ➤ We will create a folder for the exercise drawings. This can be done directly in the save window as well as in the open window:

Choose display mode, just try it!

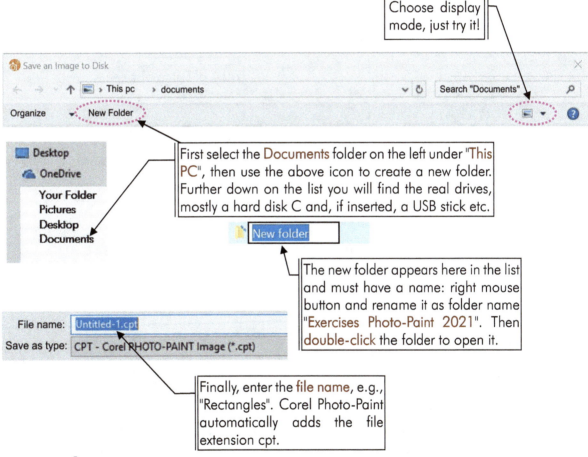

First select the Documents folder on the left under "This PC", then use the above icon to create a new folder. Further down on the list you will find the real drives, mostly a hard disk C and, if inserted, a USB stick etc.

The new folder appears here in the list and must have a name: right mouse button and rename it as folder name "Exercises Photo-Paint 2021". Then double-click the folder to open it.

Finally, enter the file name, e.g., "Rectangles". Corel Photo-Paint automatically adds the file extension cpt.

Summary:

- ◆ Select the desired folder position - New folder - Rename folder.
- ◆ Open folder with a double-click on it.
- ◆ Assign file name and close with Save or Enter.

About the Folders:

- ◆ The Documents folder (for your own work, formerly "your own files") is displayed at the top but is physically stored on hard disk C: C:/User/Username/Documents/...

  - ✋ Knowing the reallocation is important for data backup or if you want to copy your exercise drawings to a different location.

  - ✋ To avoid losing sight of your own backup work, it is recommended to use two hard drives or partition (split) the hard disk: one partition for Windows and installed programs one partition is spare for your own work.

3.4 Close File

Now we have a new image. So that the description of the file is new and can be saved completely before a file is closed.

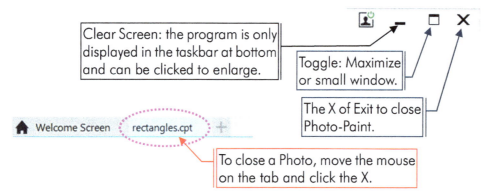

- ➢ Try out all six symbols in sequence and observe the effect.

- ➢ Close the drawing and PHOTO-PAINT. Restart PHOTO-PAINT. Open the last image, then close everything.

  - ✋ The most recently opened images are displayed in the Photo Paint in the Welcome Screen and in File/Recently Used.

3.5 Basics for New Photos

3.5.1 The File Size

In PHOTO-PAINT, we are first asked how large the new image should be, which color mode and more. Therefore, this window appears, in which the size alignment and even more can be specified:

- ➢ Resolution 150 dpi means that the image contains 150 dots per inch and therefore could not be printed on a 300 or 600 dpi printer with better quality.

dpi

> dpi = dots per inch = points per inch (one inch = 2.54 cm).

Everything can also be set later, so you could turn off this window, that appears after File/New, here. Activate again would be to select "Show new image dialog box" in Tools/Options/Corel Photo-Paint.

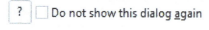

3.5.2 To Color Mode

The more colors must be displayed per pixel, the larger the file will be! If you only want to paint a black and white image, you can reduce the file size by switching from 24-bit color display to black and white, or more precisely grayscale.

Bit

♦ 24-bit color depth is fully sufficient. So as a rule, this setting only needs to be confirmed. 24-bit color depth means that 24 bits of memory are reserved per point for specifying the color per pixel.

    ↳ RGB stands for Red, Green and Blue. From these three colors, each screen and TV mixes the picture.

The following options are available for Black and White images:

1 Bit	Two colors, mostly black and white (line drawing).
8 Bit	256 Grayscales (normal black and white image).
16 Bit	65,536 Grayscales

The table shows how many colors are possible in each case:

8 Bit	256 colors (too few for Photos!)
16 Bit	65,536 colors - the usual setting for the screen display (true color).
24 Bit	16.77 million displayable colors.
36 Bit	68 billion colors (High Color).

The following formula is based on 2 high respective bit depth.

3.5.3 To Resolution

The higher the resolution is selected, the larger the file becomes:

♦ An image in A3 format with 600 dpi resolution takes about 200 MB, a DIN A4 image 50 MB in Photo Paint format cpt.

    ↳ You can test a DIN A3 image with 300dpi, then press the right mouse button and select Document Properties. The file size is displayed as the size in the working memory (66.7MB) since it has not yet been saved to data carriers. Close image and equal with 600dpi results in 210MB.

    ↳ With only one GB of RAM, this would be a problem, since all drawing steps are also cached and therefore the file becomes even larger when working. At least 16 GB of memory is recommended for professional image editing, because if the RAM is insufficient, it is swapped out on the hard drive, which makes all actions significantly slower, unless you have installed an ultra-fast m.2 SSD hard drive.

3.6 Final Exercise of this Chapter

A little routine exercise that will not cause you any problems.

➤ Close the previous exercise "Rectangles", if not already done. Start three new pictures (+ click), 640 x 480 points each.

➤ Draw some rectangles or other elements in each image (try): Briefly press and hold the left mouse button on the rectangle symbol, then the selection menu with ellipses or circles, polygons etc. is displayed. Set the colors differently in each case.

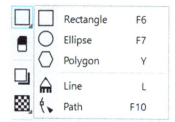

➤ When saving, first create a new folder named Test, then save the images there under the names Test 1, Test 2 and Test 3.

    ✎ Save Test 1 under Test 1 - Copy.

➤ Set Test 2 to full screen size.

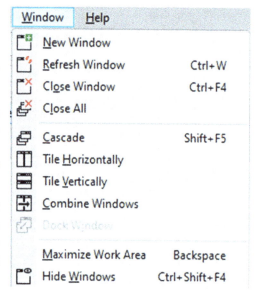

    ✎ Switch to Test 3 (click on the tab or Window Test 3).

    ✎ With Window/Cascade you can display a photo alone without the Photo-Paint command bar, with Window/Fit it is fitted back into Photo-Paint. Please try it.

    ✎ With Window/"Maximize Work Area" you get the image as big as possible on your screen, to go back click again "Maximize Work Area" or Backspace.

    ✎ Display all images e.g., Window/Tile Horizontally. Also try "Tile vertically".

➤ Close Tests 2 and 3.

➤ Position Test 1 and Test 1 - Copy so that one image occupies the left half, the other the right side of the screen: Window/Side-by-Window.

➤ Close all Images.

➤ Select File/Open and delete the folder "Test". Close the File Open window with Cancel.

This exercise was about creating, saving, copying, renaming and deleting several image files and displaying them in Photo-Paint, e.g., to copy something from one photo to another.

Notices: ....

....

....

....

4. Colors, Rectangle, Ellipse

PHOTO-PAINT offers numerous functions for painting, which are introduced in this chapter. You always need these basic drawing functions because many photos need to be reworked or modified:
Select Colors, lines, rectangles, ellipses, text and erasing.

4.1 The Drawing Functions at a Glance

➢ Start a new Drawing (1024x768pxl).

Before we start drawing - step by step - here is an overview of the drawing tools in the tool's palette on the left:

Tools

Selection Tool = Pick Tool: this selects objects by clicking on them.

Mask tools for Highlighting.

Edit existing Masks.

Cropping Image edges.

Zooming: click and zoom in with the left mouse button, zoom out with the right mouse button.

Cloning, Red Eye Removal, Retouch Brush, Repair Clone.

Smearing, at the top liquid (not by Essentials), for instance, strong at the bottom as with cotton swabs.

Write Text.

Brushes for painting and Effects.

Rectangles, Ellipses or draw Lines.

If such a triangle is available, hold down the mouse button and a selection menu will appear.

Eraser

Deposited Shadow.

Transparency

Use the pipette to capture colors from the Image.

Lines and background color including the fill color - double-click to open the respective menu.

Fill surfaces of the same color with the paint bucket.

Icons arranged differently?
Window Workspace Standard
(not available for Essentials)

Note the following Functions:

- If you do not move the mouse over a symbol for a short time, the name and a short description will be displayed.

- For functions with the small triangle, a selection menu opens when you hold the mouse over the icon shortly. For example, this allows you to switch to ellipses for the rectangular icon.

  ↳ You can set each selected tool in the property bar, for instance, the line thickness or transparency.

  Firstly, adjust, and draw because many things cannot be changed afterwards in Photo-Paint.

Remember to select the appropriate function first!

- Many beginners forget to switch to the pick tool and therefore accidentally draw many new mini objects.

  ↳ If you unintentionally draw another rectangle, for example, then immediately Undo (Undo Edit or[Ctrl]-z)!

4.2 Undo and the Redo List

Every beginning is difficult! Before you start your first attempts, here are instructions on how you can undo successful work:

- Immediately Press Edit/Undo, icon or the keyboard shortcut [Ctrl]-z.

  ↳ You can undo up to 25 actions in PHOTO-PAINT, but only in the order in which they were entered.

↺ ↻

undo

Problem with Undo:

- You want to undo an action but have since executed meaningful commands.

  ↳ You would also have to undo these actions since it only decreases in sequence! If necessary, objects can be saved by copying them into another photo before undoing.

Therefore, this is recommended for safety:

- For complex images, save them regularly under a different name: Picture 1, Picture 2 …

  ↳ If necessary, it is then possible to copy from a previous stage back to the current state.

To undo several commands, you can start a docking window in PHOTO-PAINT (works *not by Essentials* and Home & Student Edition): Window/Dockers/History.

> Not sure how something works? No problem anymore with Undo. Try, if not correct, undo immediately and try the next alternative.

Before we really start drawing, we will take a look a little more thorough at the different colors to make it really colorful.

4.3 Select Colors

Colors can be selected very easily using the color palette on the right-hand side of the screen:

- ◆ Just click on a color on the right, where applies:
  - ↳ Use the left mouse button to select the fill color,
  - ↳ select the line color with the right mouse button.

First select the colors, then draw the Object.

The color palette contains even more colors. With the triangle arrow, you can open other color palettes, with the arrows above and below the color palette you can easily move the displayed area.

You can drag and drop the color palettes at the top of the dots with the mouse, then the window size at the edges can be adjusted with the mouse.
Slide back (can be difficult, so let's practice this now) in the upper colored bar: grab it and move it back to the right edge with the mouse.

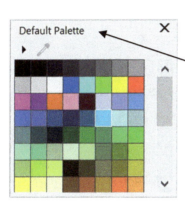

Left mouse button for the fill color, right mouse button for the lines.

The current colors are displayed at the bottom left of the Utilities palette:

- ◆ at the top, (here purple) the painting color = line color,
- ◆ below (here green) the Fill color.

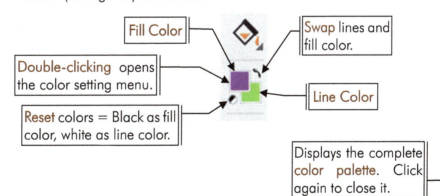

Fill Color

Swap lines and fill color.

Double-clicking opens the color setting menu.

Line Color

Reset colors = Black as fill color, white as line color.

Displays the complete color palette. Click again to close it.

- ◆ If the color palette is disabled:
  - ↳ This can be activated for Window/Color palettes, the pre-set is the "*Default Palette*".
  - ↳ Here you will also find numerous other pallets, e.g., Pantone.

4.4 The Property Bar

The most important settings for the selected command and object are displayed in this bar.

The Property bar with the selected rectangular tool:

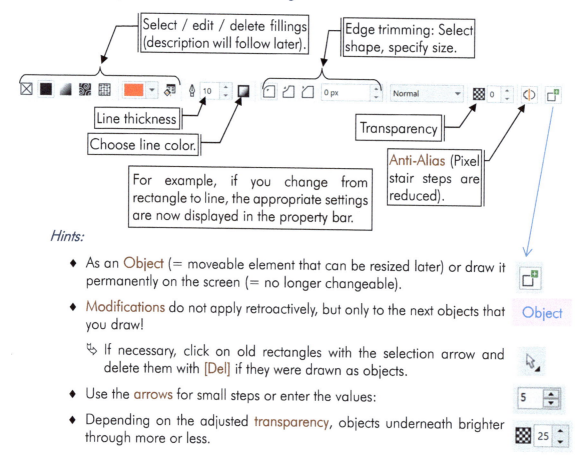

Hints:

♦ As an Object (= moveable element that can be resized later) or draw it permanently on the screen (= no longer changeable).

♦ Modifications do not apply retroactively, but only to the next objects that you draw!

☞ If necessary, click on old rectangles with the selection arrow and delete them with [Del] if they were drawn as objects.

♦ Use the arrows for small steps or enter the values:

♦ Depending on the adjusted transparency, objects underneath brighter through more or less.

4.4.1 Switch the Property Bar On or Off

The toolbars are initially arranged permanently. Click the right mouse button in the empty area of a toolbar, then you can deactivate "Look Toolbars" (not by Essentials).

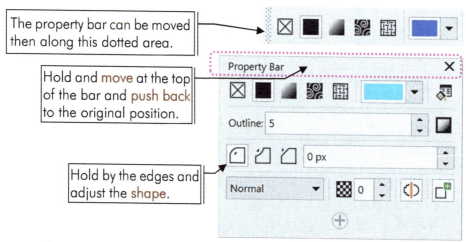

♦ If switched off, it can be switched on again in Window/Toolbars/Property Bar (check the box).

4.5 Rectangles, Ellipses

Now you know how to choose colors. And so that you can see the difference between lines and fill color in practical use, we start with rectangles and ellipses.

Line thickness

10

➢ Set a larger line thickness (in "Outline") in the property bar so that we can see the lines.

➢ Select the Rectangle tool and draw:

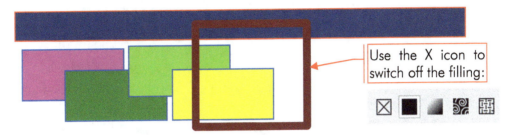

Use the X icon to switch off the filling:

➢ Now hold down the left mouse button on the rectangle icon until the Ellipse-Function appears.

➢

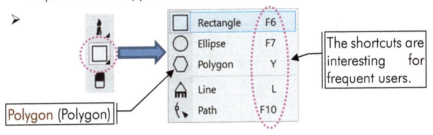

Polygon (Polygon)

The shortcuts are interesting for frequent users.

➢ Now, Draw some Ellipses:

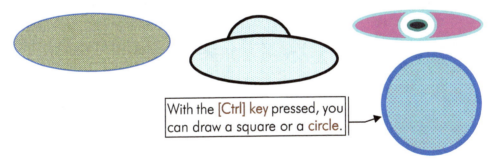

With the [Ctrl] key pressed, you can draw a square or a circle.

➢ And now a couple of Polygons:

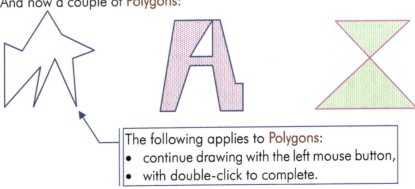

The following applies to Polygons:
• continue drawing with the left mouse button,
• with double-click to complete.

4.6 Objects

If the option "New Object" is active in the property bar, the size of the drawing can be changed later or moved with the selection arrow. Then we are talking about an object.

♦ Disadvantage: this image area is saved twice (pixel of the object and background); therefore, the file gets bigger and bigger.

↳ CorelDRAW is therefore better for object-oriented drawing:

4.6.1 Reshaping Objects

You can drag and move objects later with the Object Pick Tool or change the size at the drag points:

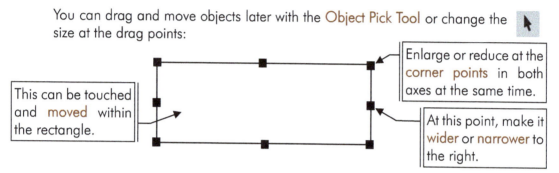

Enlarge or reduce at the corner points in both axes at the same time.

This can be touched and moved within the rectangle.

At this point, make it wider or narrower to the right.

Changes must be confirmed: Double-click on object or right-click on the object, then choose Apply.

If you press again, the Handlebar points change:

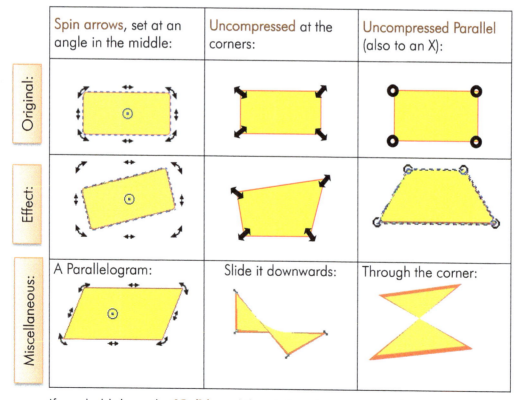

	Spin arrows, set at an angle in the middle:	Uncompressed at the corners:	Uncompressed Parallel (also to an X):
Original:			
Effect:			
Miscellaneous:	A Parallelogram:	Slide it downwards:	Through the corner:

If you hold down the [Ctrl] key while rotating, it rotates exactly: 15°/30°/45°/60°/90° etc.

4.6.2 Assign Changes

Are you stuck?

- ◆ If you have **changed** the size or other properties,
  - ↳ you must assign them by **double-clicking** on this object. Only then can all commands be selected again.
  - ↳ If you double-click on **another object**, the changes are not made but **canceled**.
  - ↳ The settings can also be changed or reset with the **right mouse button** on the object, then **apply**.

You can also select the setting option in the property bar:

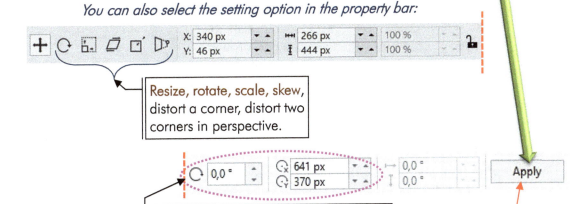

Resize, rotate, scale, skew, distort a corner, distort two corners in perspective.

Rotating is selected; therefore, the pivot point and angle can be set here.

Apply

The property bar for Scaling:

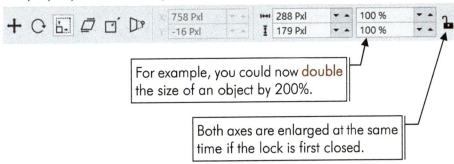

For example, you could now **double** the size of an object by 200%.

Both axes are enlarged at the same time if the lock is first closed.

For Practice:

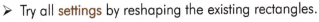

- ➤ Try all **settings** by reshaping the existing rectangles.
- ➤ Switch to the **Line tool** (hold the mouse down) and the settings in the window switch to the Line options:

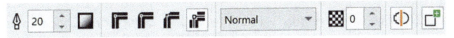

- ➤ Similar setting options are available for the **Ellipses and Polygons**.

4.6.3 Combining Objects

With the default setting in PHOTO-PAINT, you can draw freely movable objects that are detached from the screen.

This is practical for correction but sometimes annoying, for example, when erasing over the whole drawing or when filling the background. Because the eraser only affects the selected object if an object is present in the drawing.

More about that later. Right now, you should know how to merge objects with the background. It works this way:

- ◆ With the command Object/Combine... or on the Merged object right mouse button. Three options are possible:

  - ↳ Objects can be combined together if several objects have been selected previously.

  - ↳ Combine objects with background... only the selected object is merged with the background. This can also be done using the keyboard shortcut: [Ctrl]-down.

    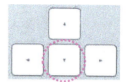

  - ↳ All objects with background: all objects are merged with the background. You can also use the keyboard shortcut: [Ctrl]-[Shift]-down.

    After merging with the background, the objects can no longer be changed! But the file size becomes smaller and the whole image can be edited with effects, for instance, the eraser, fill-bucket or distort.

- ➤ Before and after merging, press the right mouse button on our rectangle exercise photo (not on an object), then press Document Properties, and note the file size.

4.6.4 Summary of Objects

Objects (freely movable elements) are displayed when drawing, that is, if the "Objects" icon is clicked in the property bar.

- ◆ You can click objects with the selection arrow, then delete them with [Del], resize them with the selection arrow at the handle points, rotate and, move the object, etc.

- ◆ You can combine objects with the background (Merging).

  This function must be disabled or enabled separately, because each drawing tool Photo-Paint memorizes the setting even after Photo-Paint has been restarted, which is why looking at this function before the drawing is not wrong.

CorelDRAW is better suited for extensive work with Objects. Insert the photos or photo excerpts prepared in the PHOTO-PAINT and finish them with text, graphics, and effects.

5. Erasing, Pipette, Paint Bucket

♦ For deletion, there is not only the eraser, there are other possibilities:

   ↳ to undo the last actions,

   ↳ erase something away - like with a real eraser,

   ↳ Repainting is also a good possibility.

5.1 The Normal Eraser

♦ If Objects are available, only the active object can be erased or double-clicked on the eraser.

♦ If no Object is available, the entire image can be erased and *the entire image can be deleted* by double-clicking on the eraser!

You can also adjust the eraser like a brush in the property bar, options like a thicker or soft border or special shapes.

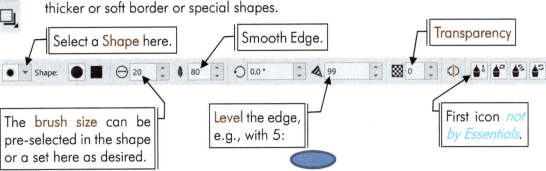

Select a Shape here.

Smooth Edge.

Transparency

The brush size can be pre-selected in the shape or a set here as desired.

Level the edge, e.g., with 5:

First icon *not by Essentials.*

With this eraser, you can radically erase everything. Try it out.

➤ First, try to erase the objects, then combine all objects with the background and erase again.

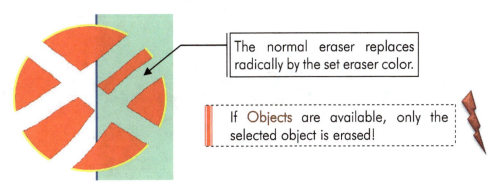

The normal eraser replaces radically by the set eraser color.

If Objects are available, only the selected object is erased!

5.2 Other Ways of Erasing

The colors offer us a practical way of erasing larger areas - simply overpainting them with the paper color.

♦ Select the desired background color as fill and line color. Either click left and right mouse button on a color of the color palette or use the pipette to select a color from the photo.

♦ Second possibility: Merge objects and draw a rectangle over the image part to be deleted. That is, Practical for erasing large areas. If necessary, deactivate the transparency.

♦ You can also paint over areas with the Brush (adjust brush size accordingly) or draw a correspondingly thick line in the color of the background.

↪ This allows even blurred edges to be smoothed.

5.2.1 Undo Brushstroke

With " Undo Brush" you can only delete or erase what you have drawn with the Brush.

"Undo brush" can be found by the Paint Tool:

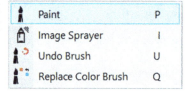

Paint	P
Image Sprayer	I
Undo Brush	U
Replace Color Brush	Q

➤ First, use the brush to draw a few strokes or objects in different colors.

↪ You will notice that the Brush has similar options as the Eraser.

➤ Select "Undo Brush" and erase. Also try erasing in other ways.

Only the last drawn brushstroke will be erased.

The underlying rectangle and the previous lines are not affected. If you want to add something to a real photo, this tool is ideal for erasing what you have drawn with the brush without changing the background.

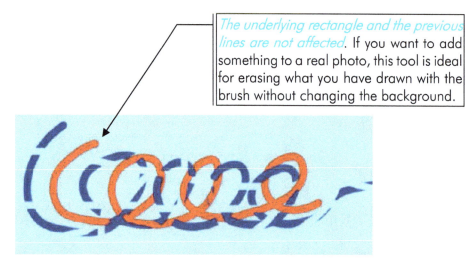

5.2.2 Adjusting the Eraser Color

Usually, you erase out and the color of the background remains white. However, you can personally change the color of the eraser. Due to the eraser color, there is practically no difference between the eraser and the brush.

Eraser Color = line color = right-click on the color palette. Fill color = left click on the color palette. The line = eraser / fill color is indicated at the bottom left, see p. 27. This does not work if objects are available, then only the objects are erased, the color of the background becomes visible.

➢ Select a color from the color palette with the right mouse button. The selected erased color must now appear during erasing.

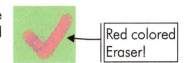

Red colored Eraser!

5.3 The Pipette

There is another very useful tool for color selection, the pipette. The pipette is extremely useful for photos because they contain far more colors than shown in the color palette.

- ♦ left mouse button: Pick up fill color,
- ♦ [Ctrl] key and left mouse button: Pick up line color.

Give it a shot:

➢ Select the pipette and take a fill and line color one after the other from the image and draw a new rectangle with these colors.

5.4 The Replace Color Brush

With the above-mentioned option to change the color of the eraser, you can change image colors with the Replace Color Brush:

➢ Draw a rectangle with a blue line and a red filling, then erase with the color replacement brush, this now replaces the red filling with blue eraser strips, since the color replacement brush replaces the fill color and only this with the line color, for further use see page 40.

If objects are present, colors are only replaced for the currently selected object, usually this is the last one drawn, if necessary, combine objects.

- ♦ In the case of real photos, the pipette is useful here to pick up the color that is to be replaced from the photo.

↳ The following applies here: simply click on the color to be replaced (fill color), click on the new desired color (line color) while holding down the [Ctrl] key.

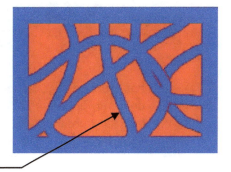

In this case, the red filling color has been replaced by the blue of the line, so that lines can be erased inside without damaging the blue frame of the rectangle.

5.5 The Paintbucket (Fill Tool)

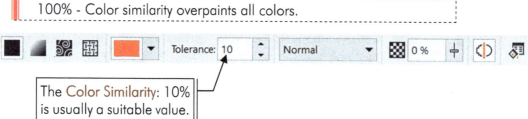

- ♦ with the Pipette, colors can be taken from the image,

- ♦ into the picture with the Fill Tool.

The Color Similarity:

- ♦ The paint bucket will be filled until another color is added:

  - ✎ in the property bar, you can specify the relevant color similarity in a percentage.

> 100% - Color similarity overpaints all colors.

Tolerance: 10   Normal   0 %

The Color Similarity: 10% is usually a suitable value.

- ♦ In practical terms, the correct value must be determined by trial and error:

  - ✎ Adjust color tolerance, fill, view, correct [Ctrl]-z and color tolerance, fill again, etc.

  - ✎ If necessary, the edge areas to be filled can also be repaired with thin lines so that excessive filling is avoided.

> If there are objects, only marked object can be filled, or all outside of marked object!

Little practice:

- ➢ Change the fill color with the right mouse button and assign it with the Paint bucket to some rectangles and slice areas.

- ➢ Two rectangles were drawn, with the larger one having the background color as the fill color with the pipette, then the smaller one was drawn in the middle.

- ➢ Then, the gap was filled with the blue paint bucket.

Pouring out Colors

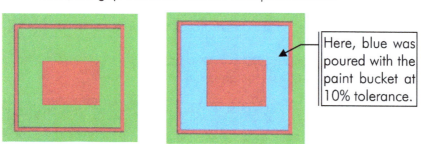

Here, blue was poured with the paint bucket at 10% tolerance.

> For example, if you zoom in on an area of a photo, you will see that uniformly appearing colors of various colored pixels are screened and that the transitions are not sharp, but run from green to light green, light red and red. This makes it difficult to work with the paint bucket.

6. Zoom, Text, and Line

We do not need to zoom in on our small pictures yet. The larger the images become, the more details are contained and the more important it becomes to enlarge image areas.

6.1 Zooming

- ◆ Activate the magnifying glass and the commands to zoom in/out that appear in the property bar but you rarely need them because they are easier to do as follows:

  ✎ left mouse button: enlarge the area around the mouse,

  ✎ right mouse button: minimize.

  ✎ If available, you can move the area with the middle button or mouse wheel pressed and held down as you would with your hand or enlarge or reduce it by turning the mouse wheel.

- ◆ If you hold the mouse on the zoom icon, you can switch to the Hand menu (Pan).

  ✎ When the hand is selected, you can move the visible image section by holding down the left mouse button.

  ✎ If you press "h" for Hand, you switch to the hand, with "z" from Zoom you can zoom in or out again.

If the scroll bars are available since only a sub-area is displayed, you can press this magnifying glass at the bottom left.

A Navigator-Window appears in which you can move the displayed image area with the left mouse button held down in a similar way to moving it by hand.

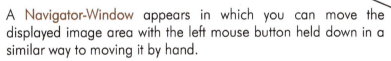

Practical shortcuts:

- ◆ [F2] = zoom in, [F3] = zoom out.

- ◆ [F4] fits the image into the window. It is a very useful shortcut, please remember it!

- ◆ With [F9]. only the image is displayed as large as possible on the screen. Editing not possible but with a mouse click of [F9] or [Esc], it will return to the previous screen.

6.2 Writing Text

➢ Start a new Image.

➢ Select the text tool and click at the position where you want to write.

➢ Select a font and size in the property bar, then write "Sample text" and save it as "Text and line".

It is best to set the text in advance:

♦ You can take the text color (= line color = left mouse button) directly from the right side of the color palette.

♦ You can adjust all other settings in the property bar.

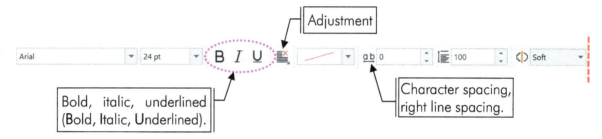

> Note: if you do not move the mouse on a symbol for a short time, an understandable description will appear.

♦ If you click elsewhere or select another command, the text becomes an object.

↪ You can edit the text again after double-clicking on it or by selecting the text tool and clicking on the text (if necessary, click several times until the text is opened for editing).

Object

↪ Change the font color in this way (see below) by opening and selecting the text with the text tool (double-clicking).

6.2.1 Converting Text

> Make a copy before editing! So, you can experiment as you want without having to rewrite the text.

➢ Activate the pick tool and observe how other commands appear in the property bar.

In the sample text, the handle points appear on the external side:

Please try everything! As with every object, you can do more:

➢ If you click on the text again with the selection tool, a rotation arrow appears instead of the handle points:

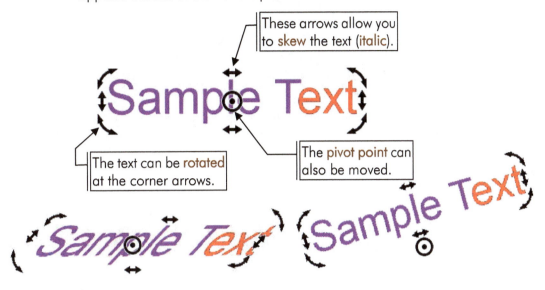

These arrows allow you to skew the text (italic).

The text can be rotated at the corner arrows.

The pivot point can also be moved.

Click on the text again and the next arrows appear and enabling the object to be pulled apart in perspective:

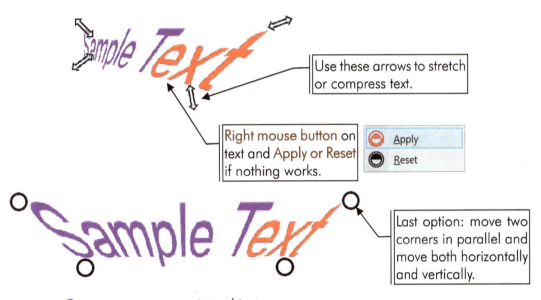

Use these arrows to stretch or compress text.

Right mouse button on text and Apply or Reset if nothing works.

Apply
Reset

Last option: move two corners in parallel and move both horizontally and vertically.

Convert or merge text into object:

◆ Right mouse button on the text and merge objects with background merges the text with the background.

    ✎ This is necessary, for example, to erase stripes with the paint replacement brush.

    ✎ However, text editing is no longer possible after this action!

Here stripes were erased with the replace color brush to create the same pattern in the text.

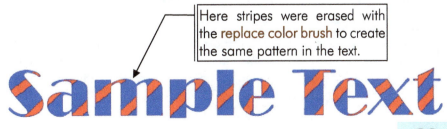

About merged Text:

♦ If the text has been merged or converted to an object, you can only change the text color with the Paint bucket or the Color Replacement Brush.

♦ Using the color replacement brush, the current text color can be replaced relatively quickly (see p. 35): use the pipette as line color to pick the current text color, then select the new color including the eraser color together with the [Ctrl] key from the color palette.

The Paint bucket is good if the text is already in combination, for instance, with an already finished photo so that the letters can no longer be marked individually and each letter should still have a different color. Each letter is cast out individually (use a new sample text):

Enlarge the text until you can see the pixel edges.

6.2.2 Practice Text

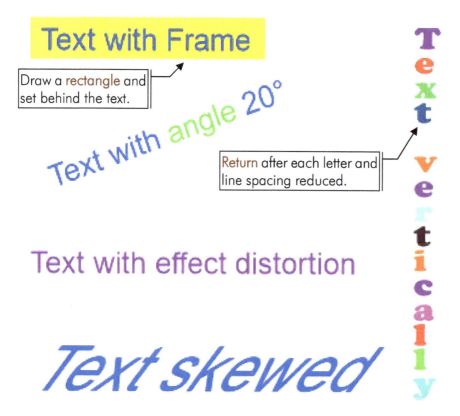

Text with Frame

Draw a rectangle and set behind the text.

Text with angle 20°

Return after each letter and line spacing reduced.

Text with effect distortion

Text skewed

Text vertically

> In general, it is recommended to only edit photos in Photo-Paint, then insert them into CorelDRAW and only add the text there, since CorelDRAW text can be edited again and better at any time and even more text effects are available in CorelDRAW.

6.3 A Straight Line

Lines this hard? You will see that lines are no longer a problem for you after you have learned the principle, the setting options, and the color options.

Lines can also be found in the rectangular menu or with the shortcut "L":

- ♦ The line thickness, etc., can be set in the property bar and the line color can be taken from the color palette (left mouse button).

Drawing Lines:

- ♦ Lines in PHOTO-PAINT are always straight lines. Freehand lines can be painted with a brush.

- ♦ A single straight Line:
  - ↳ click and hold: draw a straight line. The line is drawn as soon as you release the mouse.
  - ↳ You can also click once (=start point), then double-click (=end point) to end the line.

- ♦ Append additional Lines:
  - ↳ one quick click: Start point, move mouse away and
  - ↳ one more click: another point (can be continued as desired),
  - ↳ double clicking: Endpoint.

You can use it to draw any polygons you like. Note the option in the property bar to activate a rounded connection between the lines:

6.4 Squares, Circles, Lines in Angle

If you draw a rectangle and additionally hold down the [Ctrl] key, it automatically becomes a square.

- ♦ It applies with the [Ctrl] key:
  - ↳ instead of rectangle square, instead of ellipse a circle, and
  - ↳ Lines are drawn only horizontally, vertically or exactly at an angle of 45°.

- ➢ Draw these Lines, a Square and a Circle:

45°-Line.

6.5 Anti-Alias

At high magnification, the stair-like edges caused by the structure of pixels (dots) are visible:

The Anti-Alias* function smoothes such transitions by changing the edge pixels to produce a smoother color transition without steps.
The blue ellipse was drawn with anti-aliasing while the red one without an anti-aliasing.

*Anti-aliasing = step smoothing, image edge smoothing, contour compensation.

> ➤ Enlarge an area until the pixel grid is visible and draw two ellipses as shown above, one with anti-aliasing, one without this function and examine the differences.

Activate/deactivate the Anti-Alias function with this icon in the property bar by using the example of the property bar for the brush:

> ➤ Draw then an oblique line with and without anti-aliasing, then view both without and afterward at high magnification.

In the next chapter you will find some text where Anti-Alias is also helpful.

Note: ....

    ....

    ....

    ....

    ....

    ....

    ....

    ....

    ....

    ....

    ....

    ....

    ....

    ....

7. The Brush

The Brush is great! You can really paint with it, maybe even better than on paper. However, several variations are possible, which makes the menu seem confusing at first glance. We try to introduce this systematically.

➢ Start a new exercise and save it as a "Brush".

➢ With pressed mouse button on the brush icon, you can switch between these options which are now treated one after the other:

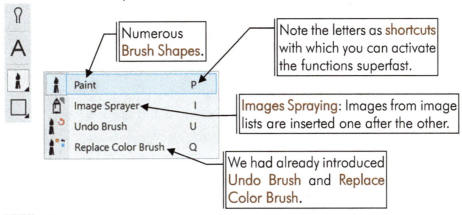

Numerous Brush Shapes.

Note the letters as shortcuts with which you can activate the functions superfast.

	Paint	P
	Image Sprayer	I
	Undo Brush	U
	Replace Color Brush	Q

Images Spraying: Images from image lists are inserted one after the other.

We had already introduced Undo Brush and Replace Color Brush.

Blurring (= effect tool) has its own icon and is an interesting addition to the brush.

7.1 The Normal Brush (Painting Color)

The setting options are extremely varied:

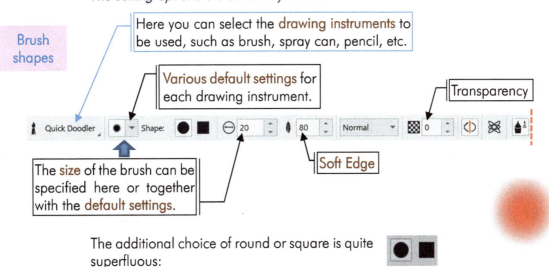

Brush shapes

Here you can select the drawing instruments to be used, such as brush, spray can, pencil, etc.

Various default settings for each drawing instrument.

Transparency

The size of the brush can be specified here or together with the default settings.

Soft Edge

The additional choice of round or square is quite superfluous:

Examples of different Brushes (each in a different Color):

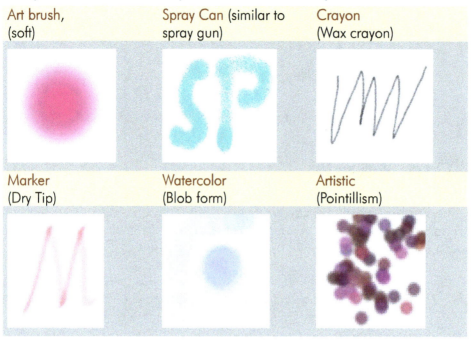

| Art brush, (soft) | Spray Can (similar to spray gun) | Crayon (Wax crayon) |
| Marker (Dry Tip) | Watercolor (Blob form) | Artistic (Pointillism) |

7.2 The Effect Tool = Blurring

Because of the similarity, this effect is described here in the brush chapter. The paints are smeared-like with a cotton swab soaked with a thinner. Give it a try!

Of course, the shape of our cotton swab can also be completely defined in the property bar, just like with the brush:

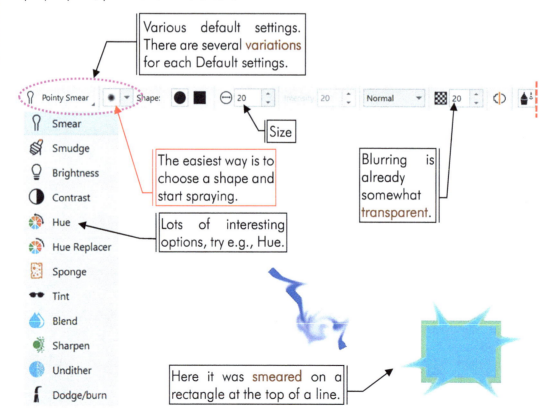

Various default settings. There are several variations for each Default settings.

Size

The easiest way is to choose a shape and start spraying.

Blurring is already somewhat transparent.

Lots of interesting options, try e.g., Hue.

Smear
Smudge
Brightness
Contrast
Hue
Hue Replacer
Sponge
Tint
Blend
Sharpen
Undither
Dodge/burn

Here it was smeared on a rectangle at the top of a line.

7.3 Exercises Brush

Now you can really paint. In practice, the Brush is well applicable. In addition, there is a possibility to paint over with white line color and to erase and smear naturally.

Such drawings can be created better and easier in CorelDRAW. Occasionally, though, something should look like hand-painted.

> In the PHOTO-PAINT, start with the background first before the small details at the end! Merging objects and save storage space but only when everything is really ready.

Try the following:

Circle with [Ctrl] key held down.

Something doesn't fit right away, undo and redraw.

Dabbed brush shape for the rocks and the reflections in the sky.

> First paint the blue background with the paint bucket, then the desert with the Brush.

> Sunrays with smearing (wide smooth coverage) and very small pin size (5 to 8).

> Paint the tree trunk with a brush, spray the leaves with a brush spray can, deactivating all color variations in the brush settings. Dab once with a large radius, then again with small ones at the ends of the branches.

> The animals can be found at the bottom of the brush by the top shape button. Just dab!

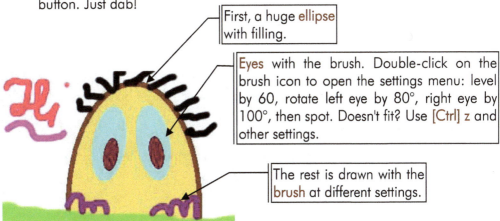

First, a huge ellipse with filling.

Eyes with the brush. Double-click on the brush icon to open the settings menu: level by 60, rotate left eye by 80°, right eye by 100°, then spot. Doesn't fit? Use [Ctrl] z and other settings.

The rest is drawn with the brush at different settings.

7.4 Image Sprayer

A very simple but extremely effective tool. With this tool we can spray images from various image lists.

Sprayed Butterflies:

With image spray cans you can also quickly create beautiful backgrounds or frames, for instance, around a portrait.

This is to be used as follows:

♦ With the Brush, the Image Sprayer (formerly: Image Spray Can) and

♦ then select an image list from the property bar at the top,

    ✍ spray them with a held mouse button or

    ✍ click once to set one image of each image series.

The property bar is used for:

Orbits will be explained in detail in the next chapter.

Here you can select the desired image list.

Transparency

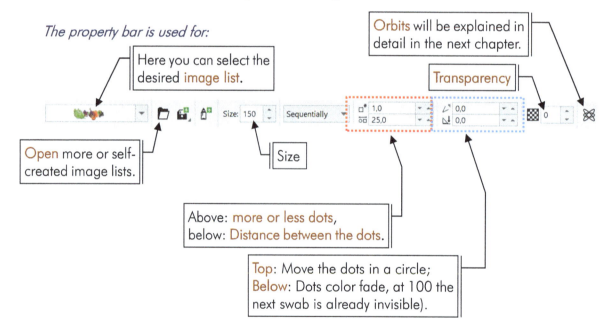

Open more or self-created image lists.

Size

Above: more or less dots,
below: Distance between the dots.

Top: Move the dots in a circle;
Below: Dots color fade, at 100 the next swab is already invisible).

Eight or more different individual images are stored with each image spray can and are inserted one after the other, for instance, eight butterflies.

Create your own Image Lists:

♦ How to create your own image lists is explained in our advanced book for CorelDRAW and PHOTO-PAINT. We are still missing the necessary masks and object commands.

8. Special Brush Settings

8.1 The Freehand Line and Calligraphy

Now let's take a closer look at the setting options. For the Brush, for example, try some types e.g., Art brush, Pencil or Artistic, then right side in menu choose a pre-set:

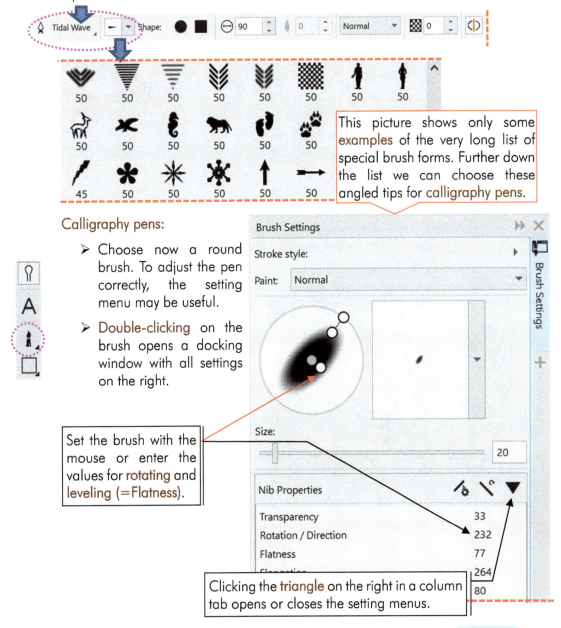

This picture shows only some examples of the very long list of special brush forms. Further down the list we can choose these angled tips for calligraphy pens.

Calligraphy pens:

➤ Choose now a round brush. To adjust the pen correctly, the setting menu may be useful.

➤ Double-clicking on the brush opens a docking window with all settings on the right.

Set the brush with the mouse or enter the values for rotating and leveling (=Flatness).

Clicking the triangle on the right in a column tab opens or closes the setting menus.

Explanation of Rotation and Flatness:

We can create or adjust a Calligraphy pen ourselves with the settings for levelling and rotating. For example, you can use it to paint Japanese characters-like with a flat brush.

Pencil shape e.g., Square   Flatness at 500   Rotation at 90 Degrees

8.1.1 Practical exercises for Freehand line and Brushes

➢ Try the following characters with calligraphy. Change the line thickness and color.

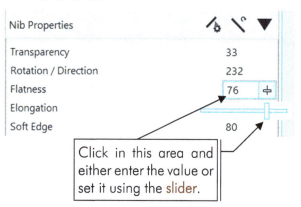

Nib Properties		
Transparency	33	
Rotation / Direction	232	
Flatness	76	
Elongation		
Soft Edge	80	

Click in this area and either enter the value or set it using the slider.

Two simple Exercises:

➢ The background was created with the Image Sprayer and the text with the Sprayer (Brush Spray Can).

➢ You can use the straight line for the house and then fill it with the paint bucket.

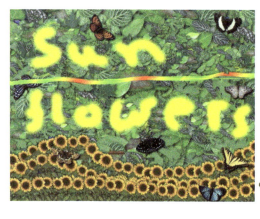

You can't paint with the mouse. A drawing tablet is recommended here.

♦ This is equipped with a pressure-sensitive pen so that the tighter the pressure, the thicker the line or brushstroke becomes.

↳ This function can be activated with the icon "Pen Pressure" located on the far right in the property bar for pen and brush (not available by Essentials).

8.2 Brush variations

The numerous other setting options are only required in exceptional cases. Therefore, a short overview is enough.

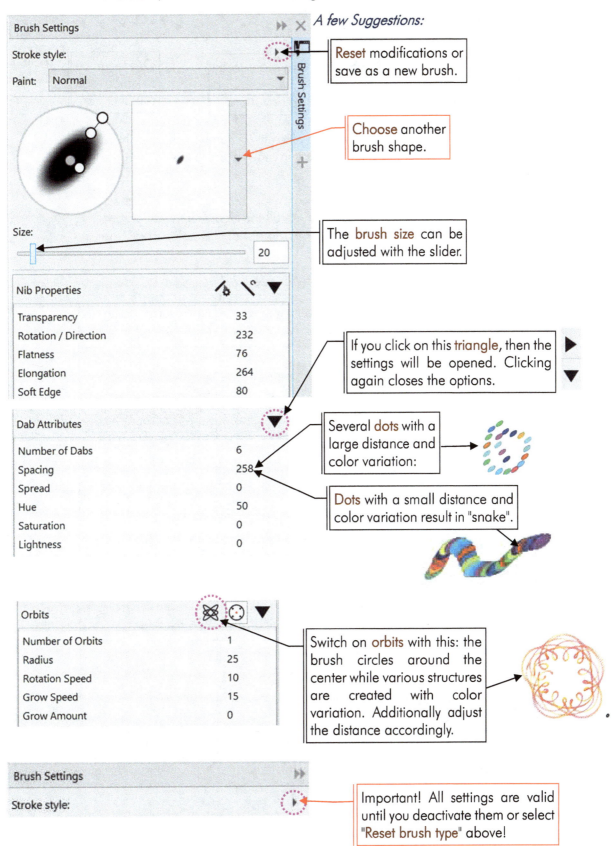

A few Suggestions:

Reset modifications or save as a new brush.

Choose another brush shape.

The **brush size** can be adjusted with the slider.

If you click on this **triangle**, then the settings will be opened. Clicking again closes the options.

Several **dots** with a large distance and color variation:

Dots with a small distance and color variation result in "snake".

Switch on **orbits** with this: the brush circles around the center while various structures are created with color variation. Additionally adjust the distance accordingly.

Important! All settings are valid until you deactivate them or select "Reset brush type" above!

8.3 Orbits

With the brush you will also find some preset orbits, e.g., Custom Artist Brushes "Wheeee!", "DNA" or "Snake":

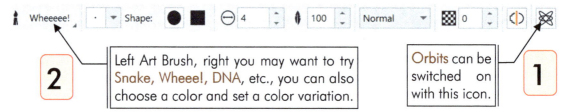

2 Left Art Brush, right you may want to try Snake, Wheeee!, DNA, etc., you can also choose a color and set a color variation.

Orbits can be switched on with this icon. **1**

Orbits can also be set manually since quite nice effects can be achieved. Here are a few hints. You will find all Orbit settings in the Brush menu (see the previous page).

Orbits become particularly interesting with color variation at color tone speed. Color variations do not apply to black and are all the clearer if the color tone range is selected as high as possible. Also, note that the color areas are calculated from the current line color.

Then you can adjust the shape of the orbits (for size 40):

One Orbit with Radius 1 and Tint Speed 100:	Three orbits with a radius of 90:	Now we're going to rotate the orbits:

Orbits		
Number of Orbits	1	3	3
Radius	1	90	90
Rotation Speed	0	0	100
Grow Speed	0	0	0
Grow Amount	0	0	0
Color Variation			
Hue Range	100	100	100
Hue Speed	100	100	100

Experiment with the speed of rotation and color:	Pen size 5, dot attributes Spacing 30:	The more orbits (here 99), the finer:

Orbits		
Number of Orbits	3	15	99
Radius	90	999	999
Rotation Speed	10	100	100
Grow Speed	0	32	32
Grow Amount	0	70	70

9. Nice Fill Patterns

A specialty of Corel are the numerous filling patterns, which we will present in the following.

➢ Start a new image, this time with 1,600 x 900 pixels in landscape format,

➢ draw a little rectangle, save as "Filling's exercise" and select the paint bucket.

The Filling-options appear in the property bar:

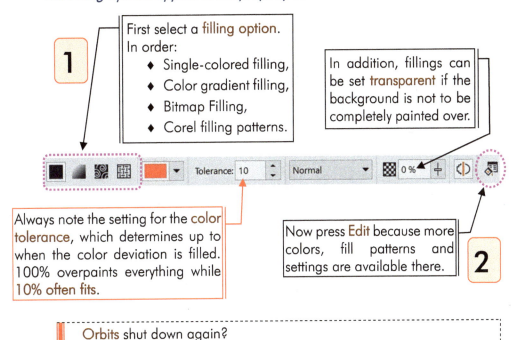

1 First select a filling option. In order:
- ◆ Single-colored filling,
- ◆ Color gradient filling,
- ◆ Bitmap Filling,
- ◆ Corel filling patterns.

In addition, fillings can be set transparent if the background is not to be completely painted over.

Tolerance: 10 | Normal | 0 %

Always note the setting for the color tolerance, which determines up to when the color deviation is filled. 100% overpaints everything while 10% often fits.

Now press Edit because more colors, fill patterns and settings are available there. **2**

> Orbits shut down again?

Because the filling possibilities are extremely numerous, we will deal with it in more detail on the following pages.

Details

- ◆ The bitmap fillings also contain real photos, e.g., cherries or stones that can be used as fillings.

- ◆ If you select a fill color, it applies to all new objects until you change the setting again.

> Changing image parts afterwards is possible with the color bucket or the color eraser, but with the restrictions for pixel graphics: depending on the color similarity, too much or too little is filled in.

9.1 Plain Fillings

A monochrome fill color can be easily added from the right side of the color palette. So, this menu is therefore only required in two special instances. Firstly, if you mix a color that does not exist in the color palette, and secondly if you want to use a color from one of the color palettes.

➢ To open the settings menu: double-click on the paint bucket or click on paint bucket and select the desired filling at the top of the property bar, then click on the "Edit filling" icon.

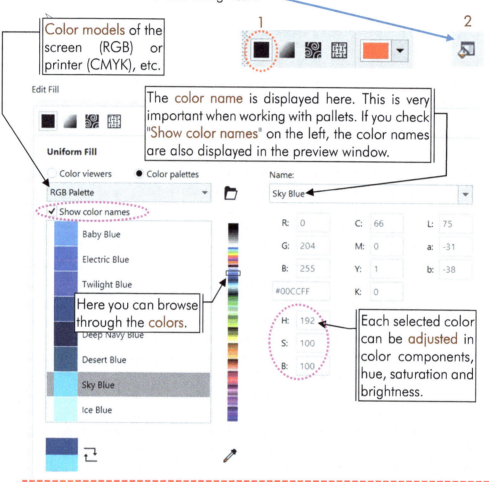

The palettes can be useful and will, therefore, be covered in detail on the next page with the color models and a brief warning.

➢ Choose a different color and draw another little rectangle.

Removing fill patterns can be difficult!

♦ A single-colored filling can be differently poured with the paint bucket at any time.

♦ But not a gradient fill, because it consists of many different colors!

    ↳ The paint bucket would only fill a small area; with a larger tolerance when the surrounding colors are usually filled with.

If necessary, press Undo immediately or save the image before assigning a multi-colored filling, or continue working with a copy.

9.1.1 About the Color Models

Some Theory. There are some color palettes to select from.

The colors on the right side of the screen:

♦ For Window/Color Palettes, you can set which color palette is displayed on the right side of the screen, usually the Standard palette (see p. 27).

Important Color Models:

In the previous filling menu, you can select different color models under "Color palettes:". A small overview of the color models:

♦ CMYK is the color model of a four-color printer, i.e. almost any inkjet printer.

> ✎ It means: *C = CYAN, M = MAGENTA, Y = YELLOW, K = BLACK.* All other colors are mixed from these four.

♦ The RGB scheme is used by monitors and televisions.

All colors are mixed from red, green and blue.

> ✎ If these three basic colors are 100% illuminated, this results in a white screen, which is why we speak of an Additive Model,

> ✎ while in CMYK, if the white paper is unchanged when all colors are off (=subtractive color mixing).

9.1.2 About the Pallets

The palettes are color combinations. Of particular interest are the standardized color palettes used by painters and printers and which existed before the computer era, for example:

♦ standard colors according to the Focoltone color scheme are usually used when painting your woodchip wallpaper.

♦ Pantone scale colors are used by printers and graphic designers to clearly describe the desired color, for instance, for company logos.

> ✎ The pallets are very important when a color has to be perfectly matched.

> ✎ Graphic artists, printers and painters have color palette catalogues. This ensures that the desired color can be reproduced accurately.

If you tell the printer the color number of a palette, the colors will match as described, except that your screen and printer will slightly distort the colors (see p. 122).

Note: ....
....
....
....
....
....

9.2 The Gradient Filling

Go to the gradient filling which is the next, more interesting alternative.

> ➢ Rectangle tool, then select on top Gradient Filling and Edit Filling... to access the selection and settings menu.

> ➢ Draw some new rectangles with different gradient fillings, e.g., linear with different angles and conical etc.

Press "Edit" to go to the setting menu:

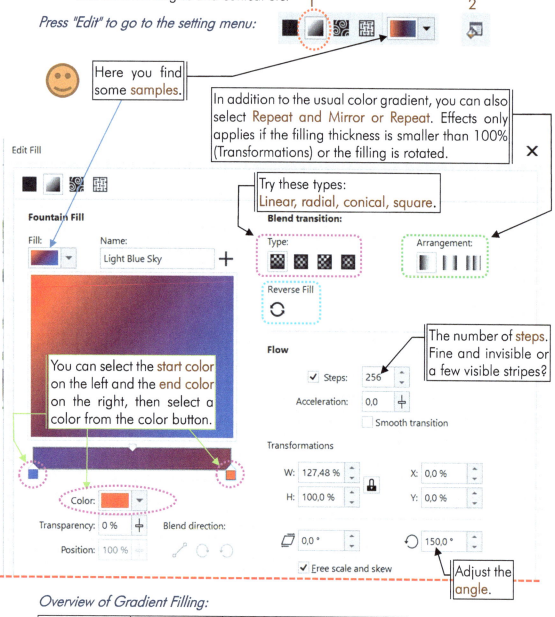

Here you find some samples.

In addition to the usual color gradient, you can also select Repeat and Mirror or Repeat. Effects only applies if the filling thickness is smaller than 100% (Transformations) or the filling is rotated.

Try these types: Linear, radial, conical, square.

You can select the start color on the left and the end color on the right, then select a color from the color button.

The number of steps. Fine and invisible or a few visible stripes?

Adjust the angle.

Overview of Gradient Filling:

Linear	Radial	Conical	Rectangle
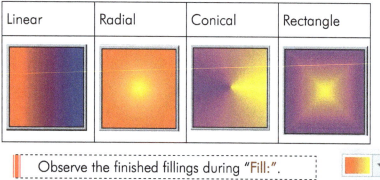			

Observe the finished fillings during "Fill:".

9.2.1 Multicolor-Filling

These gradient settings can also be used to create multi-color filling. We will try this with a little practice.

This allows you to set more than two colors:

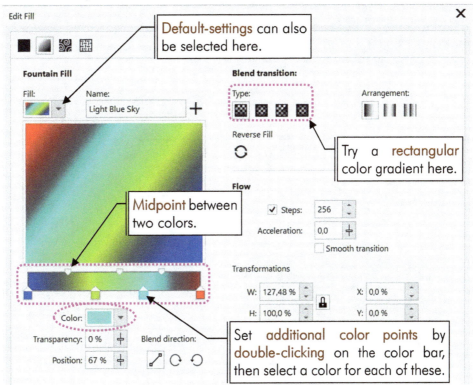

More about the gradient fillings:

- ◆ you can **move** a **selected color point** with the mouse or select another color or **delete** it by double-clicking it again.
  - ✎ You can set any number of new color points to create different fill patterns.

- ◆ With "**Angle**" you can rotate the filling or with "**Steps**" you can reduce the number of strips if specific color strips are to be visible.

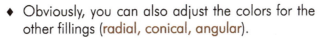

- ◆ Obviously, you can also adjust the colors for the other fillings (**radial**, **conical**, **angular**).

- ➢ **Draw** a few squares with different filling settings.

9.3 Default-settings

With this button, various default fillings can be selected. Except for these two difficulties:

- ◆ **Choose** a category (by **Essentials** only a few fillings currently available), e.g., food, and select a filling with double-click on it, now you can use it with fill tool.

- ◆ **Removing default-settings** is only possible manually: select the simplest presetting and delete the color points by double-clicking.

9.4 Bitmap Pattern Filling

From Bitmap comes the file extension bmp which was previously used for Windows background images and MS Office photos. This makes it clear that we are dealing here with a pixel filling consisting of dots with all the disadvantages such as jagged edges. The fillings shown here are scanned photos, e.g., a basket full of cherries.

> ➢ Press Edit again to select other filling patterns (or open the menu by double-clicking the color bucket).

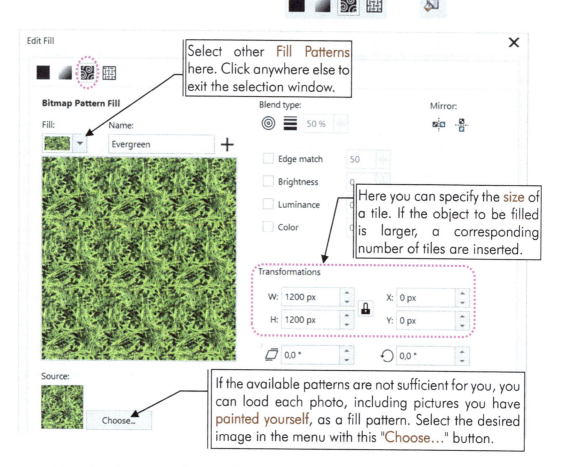

• Note that there are still many fillings on the Corel DVD and website that can also be imported. By the Home & Student Edition you have only some sample pattern fillings.   Tiling

• Since the surface to be filled is usually larger than the filling pattern, the pattern is lined up like tiles in the bathroom. If the tile is larger, only a partial area is displayed.

• Level: the next row of tiles (horizontal or vertical) is Levelled.

• Seamless: the tiles are faded over at the edges, i.e. they merge into each other.

  ✎ You can select the extent of the % button and whether it should be circumferential or horizontal or both.

Practical tip:

> ➢ Try first, then see if you need a finer or coarser pattern. Undo and adjust to fit.

9.4.1 Import Fill Patterns

A little practice:

➢ Select the button in the previous menu: [Choose...]

➢ In the Open window, select a photo on your computer.

    ✎ Your own photos should be stored in a suitable folder (with subfolders if necessary), e.g., Photos\2020, and regularly backed up to at least two external storage devices.

➢ Now this photo can be used as a fill pattern in the Corel.

➢ Use the fill tool to assign the fill pattern to the background, if necessary, adjust the tile size optimally.

9.5 Texture Fill, the Corel Filling Patterns

Now we come to the fill patterns created by Corel. Here the selection is extremely extensive. Since the images are not pixel images, the memory requirement is very low. Convince yourself!

➢ As usual, a different pattern can be selected and set during editing.

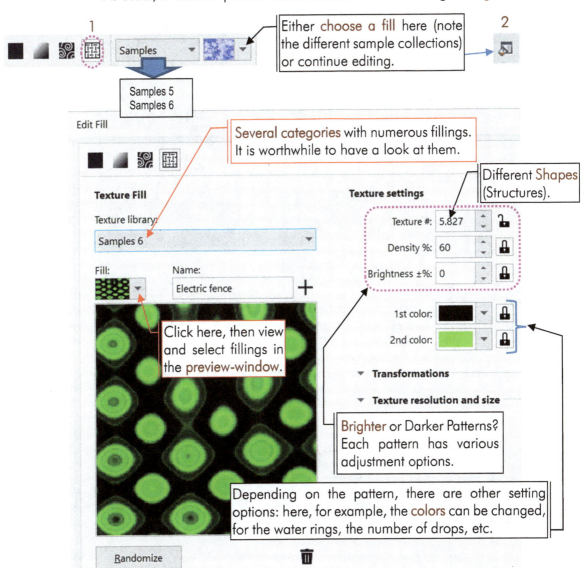

1

Either choose a fill here (note the different sample collections) or continue editing.

2

Samples 5
Samples 6

Edit Fill

Several categories with numerous fillings. It is worthwhile to have a look at them.

Different Shapes (Structures).

Texture Fill

Texture library:
Samples 6

Fill: Name:
              Electric fence   +

Click here, then view and select fillings in the preview-window.

Texture settings

Texture #: 5.827
Density %: 60
Brightness ±%: 0

1st color: ▇
2nd color: ▇

▾ **Transformations**

▾ **Texture resolution and size**

Brighter or Darker Patterns? Each pattern has various adjustment options.

Depending on the pattern, there are other setting options: here, for example, the colors can be changed, for the water rings, the number of drops, etc.

Randomize   🗑

9.6 Examples of the Fill Patterns

Finally, a small overview without the monochrome fillings:

Color gradient	Bitmap*	Texture Fill
Linear, 30 steps, 30 degrees		
Linear, 5 steps, 90 degrees		
Conical Type		
Square Type		

*Unfortunately, many bitmap fillings are only recognizable after they have been applied.

Note: ....

....

....

....

....

....

....

9.7 Practice Filling and Shadowing

A little practice with many fillings. In the PHOTO-PAINT, it is advisable to start with the background.

> ➤ New image, 800 pixels wide and 600 tall.

> ➤ First fill the paper with a gradient filling (not much of which is visible anymore in the illustration), then draw a few orbits (see p. 50) above it and blur them vigorously.

>   ↳ To make the orbits even more interesting, activate the color variation.

> ➤ Finally, write Text, tilt it, add a shadow, here "Soft down right" - then set this setting manually with the arrow and shadow progression 25 (see page 76).

With the Aid Effect for a very large brush setting.

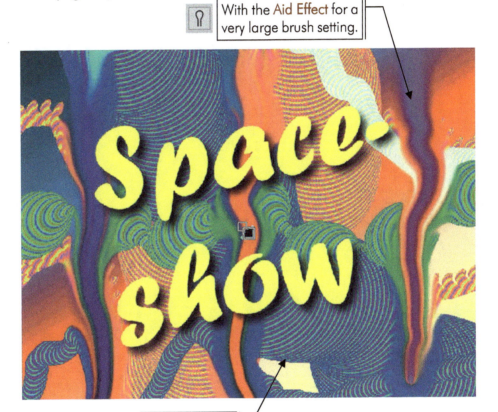

The big Orbits.

For example, you can set Orbits on the brush. By double-clicking on the brush tool, the settings menu appears in which you can obtain beautiful orbits with the following data.

The speed increase determines how fast the orbits will increase and decrease.

In the next chapter you will learn how to work with Masks and Objects in the PHOTO-PAINT.

Orbits		
Number of Orbits		50
Radius		800
Rotation Speed		100
Grow Speed		15
Grow Amount		100
Color Variation		
Hue Range		180
Hue Speed		180
Saturation Range		0
Saturation Speed		0
Lightness Range		180
Lightness Speed		180

Part Two

OBJECTS

Masked areas can be copied and pasted, creating objects in photos

All commands for Objects and Masks can be found under the menu items of the same name.

> Masks are used to mark image areas which can then be copied and pasted to make them an Object.

Icons arranged differently?
Window/Workspace/Standard
(not available for Essentials)

10. Transparency and Color Mask

Have a look at your TV guide or an advertising brochure. For us it is quite natural that excerpts, for instance, an actor from a film or a photo are set in the print media before another background - likewise product pictures in advertising brochures.

- ♦ To do this, these objects must be "cut out" from the photo. This is basically similar to cutting something out with scissors.

  - ✎ What remains is an Object that can now be placed in another photo, for instance, in an advertising brochure with a gradient filling as background.

**Objects
+
Masks**

- ♦ This is possible in the PHOTO-PAINT as in almost every photo program with the Masks.

  - ✎ Masks are selection frames that we can change until we have precisely outlined our object.

  - ✎ Only then is the masked copied and can be pasted into the current photo or into others.

What follows is admittedly not an easy matter but the day-to-day business of graphics professionals and the most fascinating way to correct, change or manipulate photos on the computer.

There are basically two ways to cut Objects out of a Photo:

- ♦ The Mask Tool: here a mask (=selection frame) is adapted as exactly as possible to the outline of the object, then everything can be copied within this mask.

- ♦ The Color Mask: often the object to be selected differs significantly in color from the background, for instance, if the background has other colors than the object. Then you can specify in the color mask which colors should be selected.

  - ✎ A quick method for special cases with plain colored backgrounds is to hide this color. The command for this can be found in the transparency tools and will be introduced soon.

> Select with Masks, then copy and paste it into the current photo or into another Object.

10.1 Select Images

Privately, everyone on the Internet will probably serve as an inexhaustible source for photos, in the professional field usually photo collections are purchased on DVD, the photos on the one hand high-resolution, on the other hand, are freely usable, but these photo collections also have their price.

- When you save downloaded photos into a folder named Photos in matching subfolders, you gradually create your own photo collection.

- You can open photos like any file from your hard drive, DVD, Connect or other external devices, directly from Photo-Paint or import or e.g., drag the photo into Photo-Paint from the Windows Explorer:

  - The photos or clip art are displayed with small preview images; in Windows Explorer, the size of these thumbnails can be set in View, the desired image only needs to be dragged into Photo-Paint with the mouse.

Photo as object:

- If you drag a photo onto an already opened photo paint image, the new photo becomes an Object in that image.

Open a photo:

- In any Internet Browser: Right mouse button on the photo/copy and then in the Corel Photo-Paint the command: File/New from Clipboard.

- In the Windows Explorer: Right-clicking/Open with/Corel Photo-Paint is the easiest way to open the photo as a separate file.

Note here:

- If you want to change the image, it is recommended to save it immediately with File/Save As on your hard disk *so that the original photo is not changed.*

- If you want to use Masks and Objects, you should save in Photo-Paint format cpt, since masks and objects can only be saved in this format.

10.2 Color Mask and Photos

In exercise, one or the other method is more suitable and this depends on the application. However, it is often optimal to approach the actual object in stages using both mask methods.

- The color mask is usually not suitable for real photos because they have too many colors with insufficient differences.

  - Unless it is being thought of when you were taking pictures. Thus, images for advertising brochures are taken from the outset in front of a clearly different colored screen.

  - Then the object can be quickly cut out of the photo with the color mask.

10.3 Hide Colors

We will explore the possibilities of the color mask with a little exercise. We will start with color transparency which can be used as the easiest way to remove objects from the background.

➢ Close all open images and photos first.

➢ Search in the internet a similar photo of the New York Skyline[1], download it and open it in Photo-Paint,

➢ Then look for an airplane photo with a blue-sky background that is as monochrome as possible, e.g., airbus beluga A300. Also download it and drag it from Windows Explorer into this skyline photo.

Now you only have to hide the background of the plane. There is a special tool for this.

➢ Switch to the Color Transparency tool for the Object Transparency tool. Now you can click on the bird's background to hide it in the simplest way.

   ✎ If necessary, click several times if a background is made up of different colors.

➢ If finished, you can copy sometimes.

   ✎ Rotate or reduce the size of the copies a bit so that it looks like different airplanes, not copies:

A completely new and interesting photo is taken.

Unfortunately, this tool often also hides colors in the object, then with the color mask, the colors can be determined more precisely.

---

[1] *This photo from www.publicdomainpictures.net*

10.3.1 Hide Colors in Other Programs

There is a command to hide a reasonably uniform background in many programs, even in most text programs.

Hide background in MS Word 2019:

- ♦ Save the image with the background as a jpg photo, load it in Word with Insert/Images, click on it, use the "Format" tools above and click on the button "set transparent color" by color, then click away from the background - unfortunately Word can only hide one color tone.

In CorelDRAW:

- ♦ An exempted Photo Paint object without background is inserted in CorelDRAW.

  - ✎ But if it would also be possible to hide the background in CorelDRAW, you can find the command at Bitmaps/Bitmap Mask (not by Essentials).

  - ✎ If it is not possible to select a color, the command Bitmaps/Convert to Bitmaps must be used in advance.

Several colors can be captured:

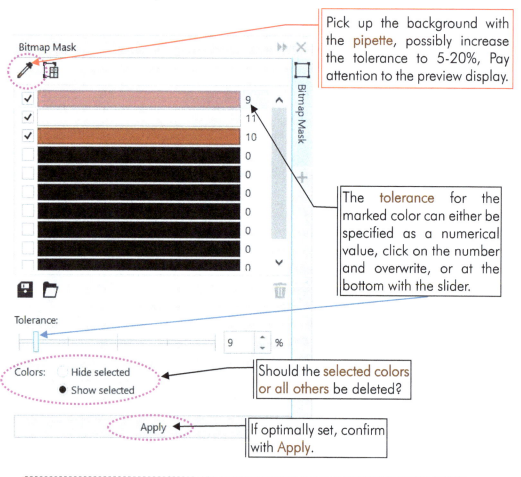

Pick up the background with the pipette, possibly increase the tolerance to 5-20%, Pay attention to the preview display.

The tolerance for the marked color can either be specified as a numerical value, click on the number and overwrite, or at the bottom with the slider.

Should the selected colors or all others be deleted?

If optimally set, confirm with Apply.

This is important because very often objects in Photo-Paint are cut out from a photo, but then used in a presentation, graphics or text program.

10.4 The Color Mask

Using the Color Mask (see CorelDRAW in the previous figure) to capture multiple colors and adjust the color sensitivity for each color tone. The mask can also be corrected later and a created mask offers another possible application.

> Do not look for the exact same rose, but a similar photo, but the colors of the flower should not appear in the background.

Let us try the following exercise:

➢ Close the previous exercise and search a photo with a blossom from top, helpful with a background in different colors as the blossom.

➢ First, it is most helpful to paint over (dabbing) with a big size brush and a color that does not appear in the flower. Then dab a little more precisely with a smaller brush. So, most background areas can be erased simple and fast as good preparation for the color mask.

☝ Undo if necessary and switch off orbits and all color variations, these are probably still activated from the previous exercises.

> Small dabs in the remaining background as well as inside the flower can also be painted over in the flower, but only very small areas, as larger overpainted areas are recognizable because the pixel pattern structure is missing as in the real photo.

Adjust the Color Mask:

➢ Select the Color Mask by Mask and use the pipette to capture several colors of the background.

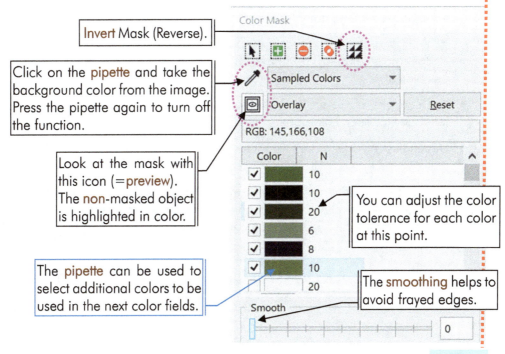

Invert Mask (Reverse).

Click on the pipette and take the background color from the image. Press the pipette again to turn off the function.

Look at the mask with this icon (=preview). The non-masked object is highlighted in color.

The pipette can be used to select additional colors to be used in the next color fields.

You can adjust the color tolerance for each color at this point.

The smoothing helps to avoid frayed edges.

Tips on how to choose a color:

- First enlarge the picture well before starting the color mask.

- Note the preview, here it helps to switch to the selection frame instead of "Overlay image".

  - If there is also a marking frame on the outside, then the edge area, not the flower, is masked, then invert the mask.

- When you pick up a color with the pipette, make sure that areas are also marked within the flower, then reduce the tolerance until these are no longer marked.

  - If this is not possible, this photo is unsuitable for the color masks, as the colors in the object and outside are too similar.

  - Other mask tools such as the freehand mask then lead more quickly to the desired result, which is described in the next chapter 11.

- Assign the mask with OK, if it has been largely set appropriately.

> It doesn't have to be perfect and it usually doesn't work with the color mask either, but we can still correct it afterwards.

Correction options:

- Eliminate existing holes inside with:
  Mask/Mask Outline/Remove Holes.

- Erase too much masked material on the outside with the brush mask at "-". A detailed explanation of this follows in chapter 10.6.

10.4.1 More About the Color Mask

- The Tolerance (Column N) is an important setting. The suitable selection of colors and color tolerances must be determined for each image through experiment, note the preview.

  - With a greater tolerance, unwanted colors may still be marked. Tolerance equal to 100 masks for all colors as if the computer were color-blind.

- You can pick up several colors one after the other and set the color tolerance for each color tone.

- Depending on the picture it is cheaper to choose the colors of the background or the desired object to be Captured.

- Frequently, you have to work with several tools one after the other, for instance, a preselection by a rectangle master, then a finer selection with the color mask which follows on the next pages.

10.5 Important Mask Icons

In the upper toolbar you will find the following useful Mask icons:

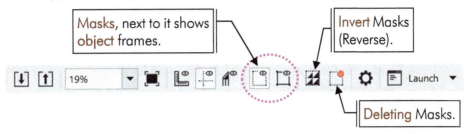

Masks, next to it shows object frames.

Invert Masks (Reverse).

Deleting Masks.

The frames for masks and objects help to recognize the existing masks and objects which aid only disable visibility briefly for viewing.

10.6 Masks Correction

A common problem with the color mask is that pixel points are not marked within the desired object, but in the background, since pixel images always consist of a mixture of brighter and darker pixels. We can correct this with " Removing gaps " or manually with the brush mask.

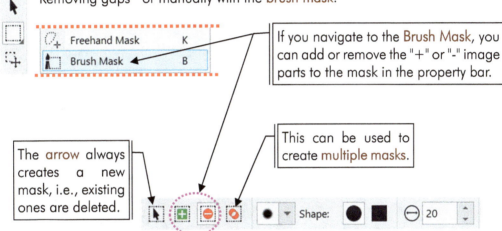

If you navigate to the Brush Mask, you can add or remove the "+" or "-" image parts to the mask in the property bar.

This can be used to create multiple masks.

The arrow always creates a new mask, i.e., existing ones are deleted.

➢ Adjust the tip shape and size of the mask brush optimally, then a mask can be corrected manually.

➢ If mask is finished, copy flower, open new image with 3000x2000 pixels and paste it there sometimes:

➢ To close all holes, you can insert again and set to background.

10.7 Mask and Effects

Once the mask fits, you can copy this area and then paste it into the same image or into other images as often as you like. Now we want to change the background color. You will see that all effects only affect the masked area.

➢ Back to the flower image with a masked background, invert mask so that the background is masked and delete it by double-clicking on the eraser (thus the mask remains).

➢ Now, fill the background with a texture fill you like and try the filling effects, that is,

 ✎ Effects/Color Transform/Psychedelic (☒ Essentials) and now

 ✎ Effects/Texture/Bubbles (☒ Essentials) and as a conclusion

 ✎ Adjust/Color Balance.

All effects are similarly simple:

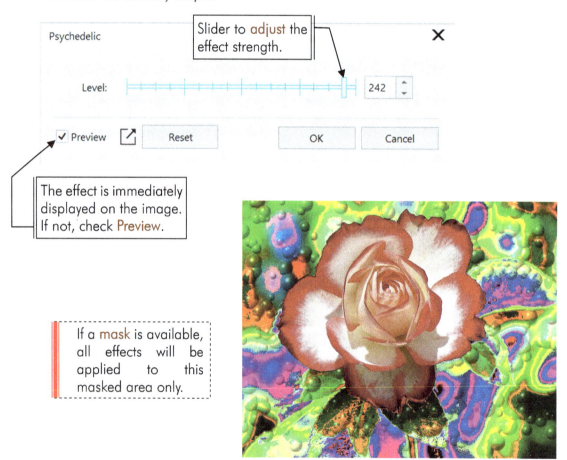

Psychedelic

Slider to adjust the effect strength.

Level: 242

☑ Preview ↗ Reset OK Cancel

The effect is immediately displayed on the image. If not, check Preview.

If a mask is available, all effects will be applied to this masked area only.

10.8 Problems with the Color Mask

The color mask can only be used for images with very few colors.

With a real photography containing a lot of colors and small differences, either not all colors can be selected or excessive selection is made of what belongs to other objects.

That is why we are trying the normal mask tools from this point on.

11. The Mask Types

You may have accidentally clicked one of the dashed rectangles at the top of the Toolbox. However, this does not draw a rectangle, but a rectangular Mask, so that this image section is selected and can be copied or moved.

11.1 Practice Rectangle Mask

Let's start with the simplest Mask.

- ➤ Search the Internet for a parachutist photo (parachutist) with a preferably single colored background and save it on your computer, then open another photo with an airplane similar to the one shown.

- ➤ Click on the dotted rectangle and draw a rectangle around the skydiver.

- ➤ Copy and paste into the plane photo. You get an object that you can move, resize and rotate.

  - ↳ Unfortunately, it should be noted that the background was also copied within the rectangle.

  - ↳ We can switch to color transparency with the icon on the left and click on the background, the result is almost perfect if the background was broadly consistent.

- ➤ But now we also want to mask the plane and then insert the plane and the parachutist into a completely different photo.

  - ↳ However, the trick with color transparency does not usually work with the airplane, because the color differences between sky and airplane are insufficient.

The skydiver has been pasted with the hidden background, re-copied and pasted twice, moved and rotated.

11.2 Masks Correction

➤ Find an airplane photo with a plain background, copy it and paste it from the clipboard using File/New from Clipboard.

Ctrl+Shift+N

➤ Use the Magic wand mask with the + activated to click and select the different shades of the sky.

♦ Problem: If a mask frame appears around the object and around the whole image, the area between object and image has to be selected.

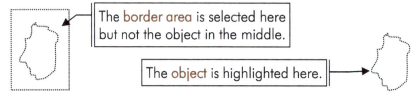

> The border area is selected here but not the object in the middle.

> The object is highlighted here.

➤ The mask can then be reversed with Invert-Mask or the icon shown on the left.

➤ Now the mask can be finished with Remove Mask Outline Holes.

Manual Corrections:

In the property bar, you will find practical icons with that we can add or remove certain areas of an existing mask.

> This is the default setting with single Mask. If you draw a new mask, an existing one is automatically deleted.

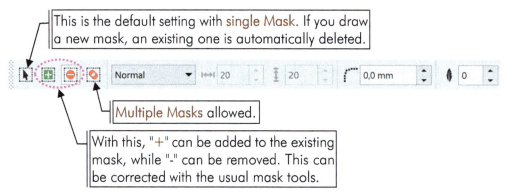

> Multiple Masks allowed.

> With this, "+" can be added to the existing mask, while "-" can be removed. This can be corrected with the usual mask tools.

With the brush mask, something can be painted or erased from the mask just like with a paint-brush. So, it is only a question of patience until the mask fits reasonably well.

➤ If the magnification is high, check the mask and, if necessary, correct it with the brush mask and "+/-".

➤ It is only a question of patience and magnification how perfect the result will be. Finally, start a new photo, fill the background, copy plane and parachutist one after the other and paste them there.

> A little twisted it looks as if the parachutist has just jumped out of the plane.

11.3 About Objects and Masks

As you can see, the jet has become an object that can be moved or resized as desired. You could copy and paste this Object into other photos as well even at multiple times.

Objects and Masks:

♦ Masks are marker frames. These frames are used to select image areas that can then be modified with effects or copied and pasted as Objects, including multiple ones.

♦ You can use the selection tool to click, move, resize, deform, and so on.

One plane thicker, the other stretched and twisted with effect/distort/swirl.

11.4 Special Masks

When objects have to be precisely separated from the background, the term "Cropping" is used in technical terminology.

♦ The masks based on color selection only work with fairly clear color differences between object and background.

♦ If this is not the case, there is a freehand mask which can be used to create a mask manually,

  ↳ as well as a pair of special mask tools, which represent a combination between this freehand mask and the color mask, but which are only advantageous in rare cases.

11.4.1 Combined Masks Tools

To get closer to the object, there are other tools that represent a combination of mask frame and color mask:

♦ The first two Masks are Marker Frames.

♦ The masks marked in blue search for color limits so that if we move halfway along the contour of the object, the contour could theoretically be recognized.

  ↳ The size of these color differences can again be determined with the tolerance in the property bar.

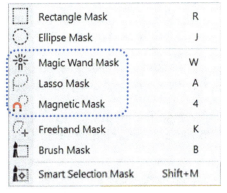

Rectangle Mask		R
Ellipse Mask		J
Magic Wand Mask		W
Lasso Mask		A
Magnetic Mask		4
Freehand Mask		K
Brush Mask		B
Smart Selection Mask		Shift+M

How these "smart" Masks work:

♦ The Magic Wand masks areas of similar color with each click.

♦ With the Lasso Mask, we are able to edge an object a little larger while Photo-Paint will search for the next inner color border.

♦ The Magnetic Mask follows color limits. If these are recognized correctly, the correct distance can be set with a click of the mouse.

> With all mask methods, + or - in the property bar can be added or removed later so that these tools can be used in a combined mode.

To practice with the magic wand and the freehand mask:

➢ Search for giraffe images in a search engine and select a photo including a free-standing giraffe (see figure next page). Save the photo in our exercise folder and open it in the photo paint.

➢ Try to mark the giraffe, for instance with the Lasso mask or Magic wand mask (+ toggle and increase Tolerance).

➢ If successful, switch to +/- and continue again.

> Usually, numerous correction processes are necessary so that we can usually mask relatively straight contours the fastest with the freehand mask.

➢ Deleting the previous Mask.

 Because the colors in a photo are not sharply separated but rather fine nuances exist; lasso, magnetic and magic wand masks are in many cases not optimally applicable so that in practice, an object with the freehand mask is usually faster released by hand than with futile attempts with these mask tools.

11.4.2 The Freehand Mask

Now we go in detail to the best solution, the Freehand Mask.

Preparatory work:

To make it easier to select the object, the image should be reduced to this object first, so that everything that is not needed is omitted.

♦ Use the Crop tool to draw a frame as small as possible around the giraffe and double-click to confirm.

> Warning! Saving would possibly overwrite the original image! So make a copy right away with Save As.

The New File from Clipboard command also proves its value time and again to get previously marked and copied areas of a photo as a separate photo.

➢ Select the Freehand Mask, enlarge head area, then click once on the neck, move the mouse until a curve appears, then click again and follow the contour of the head and continue along the other side of the neck - double click to complete.

The optimal method to draw a freehand mask:

♦ Do not draw a freehand line with the mouse button held down rather a frame with the giraffe by clicking with straight line pieces.

    ✎ Click more often for strongly curved passages, for straight sections click at longer intervals. Double-click to complete the action.

♦ Only ever approach short pieces at high magnification, then reverse on the other side and finish with double-clicking.

Let's move on:

➢ Move the image area, e.g., by panning the zoom symbol to toggle to + and select the next piece:

    ✎ After the head, add the neck, then the body, then the legs to the mask.

➢ In the end, remove overmarked areas from the outer surface, for instance, with the mask brush. Therefore, a partial area can also be enlarged.

The difficult head was selected quite precisely with a few clicks. Then move the image section and mask the next section with "+".

➢ When completed, copy and paste into an aircraft image, for example:

11.5 Exercise Poster with Objects

➢ Open a new image in landscape format with 1600x1200 pixels and apply a radial gradient.

➢ Look for a similar or suitable aircraft image, mask the aircraft with the freehand mask, copy and paste into the new image, resize and rotate.

✎ When done, right-click-assign, then duplicate objects, flip this copy with Object/Turn/Horizontal and move the copy to the other corner.

✎ Then select both planes and duplicate the object, then turn over the object vertically and move the copies upwards.

11.5.1 Text with Shadow

➢ To edit the Text afterward, click on the text tool, select it (e.g., double-click) and set it appropriately in the property bar and select a color.

You can add a shadow with the icon on the left:

➢ Click on the text, then select the icon and while holding down the mouse button, set the shadow direction on the text.

✎ Then select a different shadow shape in the property bar, for instance, as in the illustration "Medium Glow".

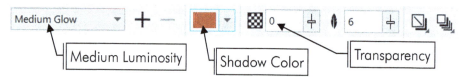

11.5.2 Ellipse Mask

We have some other mask tools we want to try out. We want another image of a meal on our poster.

➢ Search on the Internet, for instance, for "Main Dish", then open a similar dish in the Photo-Paint; right mouse click on it/copy and in Photo-Paint then File/New from the clipboard.

➢ Hold the mouse on the mask rectangle so that the menu bar will appear, then select the ellipse mask and mask the soup.

➢ At first attempt, it fails! So, therefore switch to the "Mask Transform Tool" underneath and correct the mask accordingly.

   ↳ Clicking again changes to distort, rotate, etc. as with objects, allowing the mask to be optimally adjusted. If this does not work, you must probably press the right mouse button/apply again.

➢ If necessary, use a large brush mask and + with a cautious click, that is, to pick up a lower cupcake or protruding leaves or cutlery.

➢ Copy and paste into the image, resize and arrange.

➢ Finally, use the paint bucket and Undo to try out other fillings for the background, for instance, a freely adjustable radial gradient fill from our previous illustration.

11.6 Save Masks

You can save the image in PHOTO-PAINT format cpt and thus retain the objects so that later changes are possible.

Even laboriously created masks can be saved. These options are available for mask storages in the menu Mask/Save:

Saving Masks

   ♦ Save Mask to Disk: the mask is stored on the hard disk and is therefore available in every other drawing, e.g., to cut dolphin shapes out of other images.

   ♦ Save as Channel: the mask is saved in the current image and can be loaded into it at any time if you want to copy the object again later.

   ♦ By Mask/Load, saved masks can be activated.

      ↳ Interesting: if you load a mask and the "+" is active, it will be added to an existing mask, deducted at minus.

> With the possibility to save masks, several masks can be used in one image.

   ♦ Save as alpha channel should also be mentioned for completeness. To do this, first create a new alpha channel in the menu Window/Dockers/-Channels with middle icon on bottom or the small arrow at top, then the mask can be saved to this channel.

11.7 Other Mask Commands

The following options are very useful:

♦ Mask-invert: if you have masked an object, you can use it to invert the mask to the rest of the image and delete this background or apply an effect to it.

♦ The icon to the right: Delete Mask.

In Mask/Mask Outline are still useful functions:

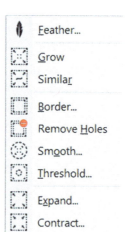

♦ Gradient: add a soft edge (gradient) to the mask.

♦ Grow: expand the mask to adjacent areas with similar colors, "Similar" adds similar colors throughout the image.

♦ Border: only a border strip whose width and transparency can be specified is marked.

♦ Remove Holes: Holes inside the mask are added to the mask.

♦ Smooth: The edges of the mask are rounded.

♦ Threshold: reduces the mask a little.

Masks visible or invisible:

The following two icons can be used to set the selected frames of masks or objects to visible or invisible.

♦ Visible is recommended for masks, as invisible masks can cause problems during editing, but it is good for previewing to make the masks and objects invisible for a short time:

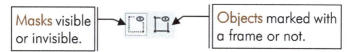

11.7.1 Mask Preview

There are two ways to display masks in the Mask menu:

♦ With Mask Overlay, the non-masked area is colored and is suitable for preview,

♦ but the Mask Marquee is better for editing a mask, it can also be activated with CTRL-H.

Also, interesting as well:

♦ Float: the masked area can be moved including the mask.

 ↳ When you copy and paste, the masked area is cut out and the background, when moved, leaves a white spot. Possibly. Undo immediately, if necessary.

11.7.2 Delete Masks

Complex masks should be saved in between, as surfer1, surfer2 etc. But how could such unneeded masks be deleted later?

Masks saved on the data carrier are normal files and can also be deleted, but not saved as channels.

[Ctrl]-
[F9]

> Save the giraffe mask again as a channel named "Giraffe1" and open the docking window: Window/Dockers/Channels.

Each computer screen consists of the three basic colors red, green and blue (RGB), that is why you will find here besides all colors (RGB) three channels for the red, green and blue color components and of course your mask as well as the saved mask.

> Click on the Mask.

Channels can be faded out or inserted on the checkbox. The active channel is highlighted in red and cannot be hidden.

RGB for all three basic colors, then individually separated as color channels: *red, green and blue*.
A click on the eye in front of the green channel disables the green color components, a click on "Green channel" only shows green.

The currently available Mask and the one saved as "Giraffe1" channel.

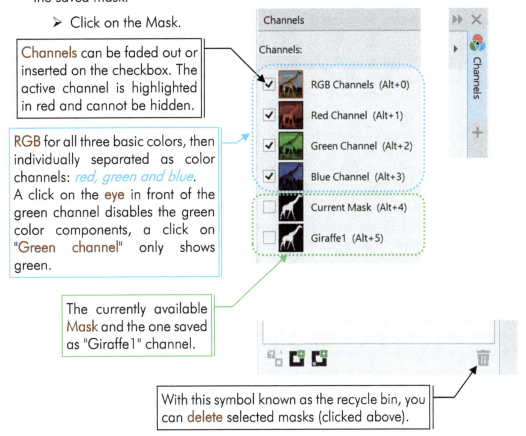

With this symbol known as the recycle bin, you can delete selected masks (clicked above).

11.8 Share Photo

For example, if you want to send a photo over the Internet, you can make a copy in jpg format as follows, which can significantly reduce the file size:

jpg

> First save cpt in Photo Paint format, if you want to keep the masks and objects, then save with File/"Save as" as file type jpg.

  ↳ In addition, the resolution or size could be reduced with Image/Resample in order to further reduce the image if necessary. Of course, save only with the jpg copy!

12. Masks and Text

Masks can be used not only to copy objects from one image to another but also to create special effects.

The principle:

♦ If Masks are present, effects only affect these masked image parts!

♦ Text is first and foremost an Object. However, we can convert objects into masks and vice versa.

  ↳ Consequently, a mask in form of the text can be created from text in order to change only the text or only the background, e.g., to make it lighter.

  ↳ To edit anything including the text, invert the mask so that the rest of the image is highlighted.

12.1 Text Position

➢ Search for "bigben" on the web and download a similar photo as shown on next page and open it in the Photo-Paint.

➢ Write the text: Language and Travel separately, choose a thick font from the beginning and set it to approx. 100pt size and turn it by 90°.

cpt

➢ Save as "language travel" so that you wouldn't have to rewrite the text in case of mishaps, save cpt in Photo Paint format because only then the masks will be saved!

➢ The Object/Align and distribute/Align and distribute command allows you to center elements - horizontally, vertically or in both axes. In our case, we only center horizontally.

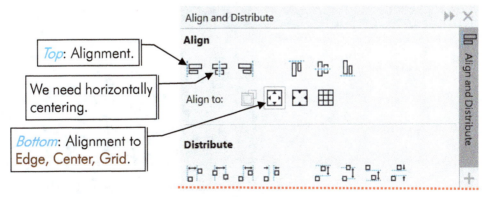

Top: Alignment.

We need horizontally centering.

Bottom: Alignment to Edge, Center, Grid.

12.2 Creating a Mask in Text Form

We now have the image and previously the text.

> ➢ Select both texts while holding down the [Shift]-key, then select Mask/Create/Mask from Object (or [Ctrl]-M).

This creates a mask in the form of the text. We can now delete the actual text.

> ➢ If you move the text a little, you will see the mask behind it. Delete both texts with [Del] because they are still highlighted.

> ➢ Save this mask to a data carrier for later use.

Why save the Mask?

> ♦ With this mask, we can now try out any effects or copy the text as a mask into a new image.

> ♦ We can start over at any time by reloading the photo from Connect and then reloading the mask. Undo would be possible but not after a photo has been saved or closed and reopened.

For example, try the following:

Effects are only valid for active masks!

> ➢ You may apply: Effects/3D Effects/The Boss…, while greatly increasing the value for height and width.

> ➢ Now try it again: Effects/Color Transform/Psychedelic.

The boss-effect creates the spatial shadow, psychedelically changing the colors of the original image so that the text is now clearly visible without completely covering the image:

Unfortunately, the effects are not available in the Essentials edition. Alternatively, you can use color modifications from the adjust-menu.

12.2.1 Relief

With the mask we can cut out the background in the form of text.

> Assign a new picture 1600x1200 crosswise, the paint bucket and a flower filling. Language Return – a 'trip' with 400pt font size at the center, then apply for 3D effect relief, while greatly increasing default values.

> Create mask from object, then save this mask to the data carrier.

Effects are missing in Essentials

> Find a photo of the French flag on the web (or paint it from three rectangles), copy it, open the new image in the photo paint with 1600x1200, paste it there, resize it and combine it with the background.

> Load the mask, copy the flag, switch to the previous photo and paste - which is more interesting, relief or with the national colors?

12.3 Create a Fill Pattern

Another variation is to create a fill pattern from a photo.

> Close all images, search for "kangaroo sign" on the Internet, download and open a photo similar shown next page.

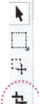

In order to use the photo as background filling optimally, we will reduce it first. The filling should finally be tiled from several small images which can be used, for instance, as a background for internet pages.

> Use Crop Tool to reduce the image to the Kangaroo Shield.

> Select: Image/Resample.

Use this command to reduce the image size:

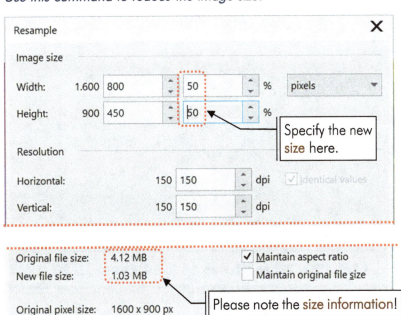

Now we can save the resized image under a different name for use as a fill pattern:

- ➤ File/Save to and in your Exercise Folder in jpg format with a file name as "Background Kangaroo".

- ➤ Then take up an orange tone with the pipette as both line and fill color, wipe away the black lines and the sky with the brush.

- ➤ Different shades of color remain, with 25% color tolerance pour out the fill color.

- ➤ Image/Resample: Resize the height/width of the image to square (maintain aspect ratio, turn off).

- ➤ Save again - we can load this new image as a fill pattern at any time.

New image for the Filling:

- ➤ Open a new image with 1280x1024 pixels in landscape format,

- ➤ Select the fill bucket and switch to Bitmap Filling in the property bar and click the Edit icon,

- ➤ then browse, select our currently saved fill image (switch to jpg file type) and pour out with the paint bucket.

- ➤ Undo, resize the tile and pour it out again.

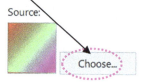

Complete the Image with Effects:

- ➤ Rewrite text, convert to mask, delete text and embellish it with effects, e.g.,:

  - ↳ the 3D effect "The Boss" and Image/Adjust/Color Balance which will change the colors.

A white rectangle has been drawn and set in the background.

12.4 The Connect Content

Many objects (cropped people, animals or objects) and photos that can be inserted into new images which are available on the Corel website. You should, therefore, take a look at them, as you can save a lot of work if you can use a finished object instead of cutting one out of a photo by yourself.

♦ You can find them in the Connect at Window/Dockers/Connect Content.

A search word can be entered here, e.g., koala.

The vector drawings from CorelDraw are converted into pixel images in Photo-Paint, this takes some time.
There are also many photos in the lower part.

Notice the scroll bar on the right.

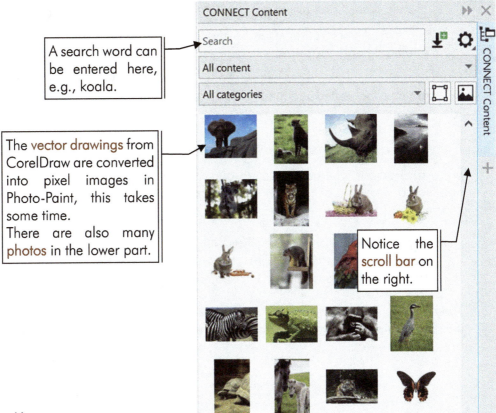

Use:

♦ If you drag a photo into an open photo with the mouse button pressed, it will be inserted into the photo as an object,

♦ or drag onto the tab bar at the top to open it as a new photo.

♦ If you want to use the objects in other programs, you usually have to hide the background with a color mask.

♦ "Get More", under "Start" or in the menu above, can also be selected with the download arrow.

     ☞ A window appears where additional Corel products may be purchased: other programs, clip art and photo packages, fill patterns, etc. with changing content.

     ☞ Unfortunately, only for a fee, because as a Corel Oldi you wistfully think back to the times when, depending on the version, around 20,000 to 30,000 clip art were added to the Corel program package free of charge.

Trick for the vector graphics:

♦ We cannot insert the drawn clip art from the top to the middle of the list directly into Photo-Paint, an error message appears. There is a trick to this: first open the desired object in Corel-Draw, enlarge it there and then simply take a photo, which turns the clip art into a photo.

   ✎ Taking a screenshot is possible with Corel Capture (included in the CorelDraw program package) or even more conveniently with the free graphics all-round program IrfanView.

   ✎ In the latter program, the function can be found under Options/-Photograph or opened with [Ctrl]-c.

Mostly the selection fits over a rectangular mask and "copy to clipboard", then this can simply be pasted into the Pho-to-Paint file.

Create your own object collection:

If you save objects, you have created yourself or the original images with the masks in a special folder, you will create your own object collection in due course.

> If you want to display all objects with the drawing merging, the file becomes much smaller, but the objects can no longer be edited. Better to store finished projects on DVD, cloud storage or external hard drives.

The PHOTO-PAINT effects are introduced in the next chapter. First, we look at the possibilities of assembling pictures. This also gives us the very nice transparency effect.

Notices: ....

....

....

....

....

....

....

....

....

....

....

....

....

....

....

13. Overlay Images

Now we will put two or more images in one and overlay them with different methods, for instance by transparency so that one image is visible e.g., in the upper left corner and gradually the other image appears in the lower right corner.

13.1 Merge Images

➤ Open two or more photos similar to the practice photos, from connect or search the internet for *lorry* or *truck* and *airplane*.

↳ If you drag a photo onto an already opened one, it becomes an object in this photo. We don't want that now! Therefore, both open as new photos, e.g., copy the image and paste with File/New from clipboard into Photo-Paint or drag here:

↳ However, optimal results can only be expected with images of the same size and same alignment, both portrait and landscape. If necessary, reduce one image to the size of the other: right-click on the document, then properties to get the current size, then rebuild the larger one with Image/Rebuild image.

➤ With this command, several images can be merged: Image/Stitch.

↳ First select "Add All" or the desired images with "Add", then click OK to open the next window.

↳ Create objects: Pictures can be moved later.

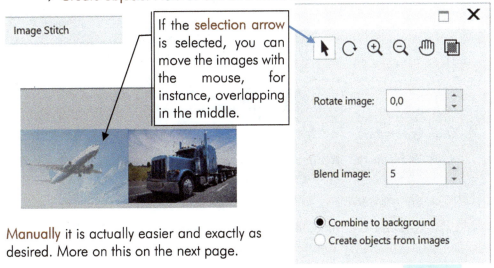

Image Stitch

If the selection arrow is selected, you can move the images with the mouse, for instance, overlapping in the middle.

Rotate image: 0,0

Blend image: 5

● Combine to background
○ Create objects from images

Manually it is actually easier and exactly as desired. More on this on the next page.

13.2 Assembling Images Manually

You have more customizable settings if you perform the operation manually and not with the previous menu command. We'll try that now.

There are multiple methods:

♦ You can use rectangle masks to copy a part of each image and paste it into another new image.

♦ With Image/Paper Size, for example, the width of an image can be doubled and the other image can be placed in the newly created location.

➢ The airplane's image size was adjusted with image page size.

➢ Then the truck image was copied and pasted to the plane,

➢ a transparency as a transition between the two images.

For positioning: An image can also be moved with the mouse in the preview window.

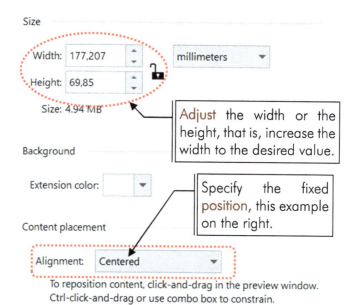

Adjust the width or the height, that is, increase the width to the desired value.

Specify the fixed position, this example on the right.

To reposition content, click-and-drag in the preview window. Ctrl-click-and-drag or use combo box to constrain.

> For transparency, detailed Information will be provided on the next page.

Useful commands:

➢ You can get information about the image by right-clicking on it and selecting "Document Properties".

➢ Images can also be cropped with the icon shown on the right:

↳ Draw the frame, resize it and complete with a double-clicking on the image, then save it as a new image with "Save file as".

13.3 Transparency

With transparency, images can merge into one another. We first need two photos of the two.

    ✎ Search the internet for diver and horses and select similar images, download them and open in Photo-Paint:

    ✎ Copy and paste the diver image on the horse image. Now enlarge the diver photo to the right until it overlaps the horse picture completely.

    ➢ Click the Transparency tool and drag an arrow at the desired image border.

    ✎ You can then move this transparency arrow with the mouse to create perfect transparency.

About the Transparency Arrow:

♦ At the beginning of this, the upper image begins to become transparent,

♦ in the middle, (this can also be adjusted with the slider in the middle) it is semi-transparent and

♦ at the end of the transparency arrow, only the lower picture can be seen.

♦

Select object transparency in this menu.

The transparency can be set at the handles of the transparency arrow (rotate, size of the transition).

Longer arrow, longer transition, short arrow = hard transition.

Once the transparency is applied, you can set it in the property bar. Try a few options:

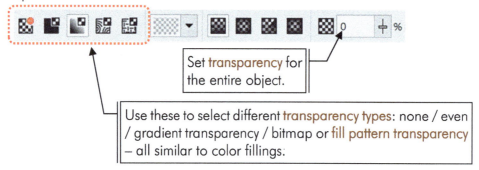

Set transparency for the entire object.

Use these to select different transparency types: none / even / gradient transparency / bitmap or fill pattern transparency – all similar to color fillings:

The same image with fill pattern transparency:

More about the Transparency:

♦ The default setting is colored gradient transparency (fountain transparency).

♦ The leftmost icon allows you to remove transparency if the correct object is selected and transparency has only been applied once.

  ✎ Otherwise Undo or Delete and insert object.

♦ If a Mask is available, the transparency is only applied to this masked area. Delete masks if necessary.

♦ You can also achieve transparent border areas with the Object/Feather command.

Activate/deactivate the Preview to check the effect. The width usually needs to be increased significantly.

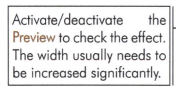

13.4 The Merge Mode

If an object is available, an interesting overlay effect can be achieved with this command. This allows you to select certain variants of how the colors of the two images (one image as an object above another) are to be mixed. This creates interesting effects.

➤ Open a photo from connect and drag a second one with the same format over it, this is our object Right-click on the object and select Object Properties:

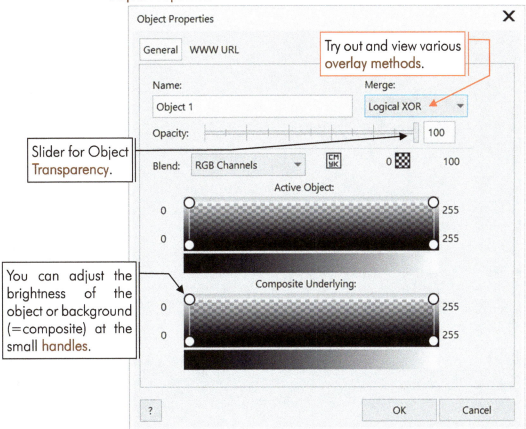

Interesting new mixed images can be created with this method, for instance, here a dolphin for Dubai skyline with XOR:

Part Three

EFFECTS

Photos can be altered or transformed into works of art using effects

---

These are divided into the menu items Image, Adjust and Effects. Unfortunately, the Effects menu in the Essentials edition is empty.

> If masks are available, image effects only apply to the masked areas. This allows Masks to be used to change only parts of an image with effects.

If you want to apply effects to the entire image but want to preserve an existing mask, the easiest way is to save the mask as a channel. Then you can temporarily remove the mask and apply the effect to the entire photo.

The same procedure applies to Objects. Save objects separately, then delete them in the current image if necessary. An alternative is the Objects or Masks Docker, in which you can temporarily hide objects or masks.

Note on the Images:

There are numerous settings and variations for almost every effect. For the images, settings were usually selected in which the impact of the effect is particularly evident. Therefore, if you apply the same effect, there may be little or no effect at the beginning. Use the sliders and settings to make the experiments.

Icons arranged differently?
Window Workspace Standard

Chapter

14. Changing Images

Another important area of application of PHOTO-PAINT is to change images, that is, to cut off image edges or to reduce an image in order to save storage space.

- ◆ Scanned images often require reprocessing:
  - ✎ Cut away superfluous edges, remove static (e.g., the pressure points of a daily newspaper), correct brightness...

- ◆ Modifying images artistically, e.g., blurring like painted, fisheye, inverting colors etc. is described in chapter 16 for effects.

PHOTO-PAINT offers numerous tools for such purposes, which fortunately are very easy to use and always follow the same pattern. Unfortunately, not with the Essentials edition.

We start with the functions that are most needed in the exercise and you absolutely should be familiar with these functions.

14.1 Resample

This function allows you to increase or reduce the size of the image file, last previously often required for images that had to be scaled down for the Web.

Resolution or Image Size:

- ◆ The same result is achieved whether you reduce the Resolution or the Image Size.
  - ✎ The size in cm is of little interest for a digital photo, since it can be scaled as required for printing.
  - ✎ The only important thing is the actual number of pixels which determines the actual quality and therefore also how large the image could be printed without the pixels. In this case, the blurring or steps becomes clearly visible.
- ◆ In the past, enlargement was only reserved for special programs e.g., PhotoZoom or Sharpen.
  - ✎ Since the 2020 version of CorelDraw and Photo-Paint, several intelligent image enlargement methods have been added so that photos can actually be improved.
  - ✎ Photo-Paint recognizes the edges and refines them, the degree of smoothing can be selected. Depending on the initial photo, the optimal setting can be determined by trying it out.
  - ✎ Unfortunately, this function is not available in the Essentials edition either.

14.1.1 Exercise Resizing an Image

➤ Search for "p51 mustang" on the web, open a photo of the silver P51, which is on the airbase and shows the pilot with the cockpit open, copy it and paste it into the photo-paint with File/New from clipboard.

➤ First look at the cockpit with the pilot in full screen and with [F4] as large as possible, note the steps through the pixels.

➤ Select: Image/Resample and increase the image size by 500%.

➤ Unfortunately, the preview does not go immediately, after OK again look at the cockpit enlarged: photo improved? The effect can be tracked with Undo/Redo and [F4]. Finally undo.

➤ Now rebuild the picture again with 500% and "Photorealistic" and maximum noise reduction of image (set on the slider) - wow, after a short waiting time the photo has become really sharp.

An exercise for reducing the size of a photo, e.g., if it is to be used on a website, can be found on page 83, another possibility of only cutting off the edges of the image on page 74.

However, images cannot be arbitrarily enlarged in size:

➤ If you enlarge the cockpit, you see that the pilot has almost no mouth.

    ↳ Details that do not exist in the original cannot, of course, be conjured up when enlarged, if this photo e.g., should be printed sharply on poster size, are noticeable.

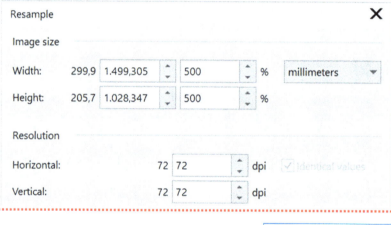

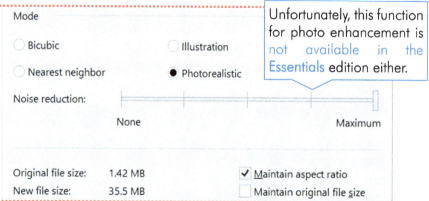

Unfortunately, this function for photo enhancement is not available in the Essentials edition either.

Determine suitable settings by trial and error. With Undo / Restore the result can be compared with the initial state.

14.1.2 Compressing with the jpg format

The jpg file format is the best way to save storage space:

- ◆ For example, If you want to use an image that is too large on the Internet,

  jpg

  - ✎ Select File/Save As and specify jpg as file type.

  - ✎ For Quality check: **High-quality** compresses almost without quality loss about 10 times and at low quality, therefore, the image is significantly poor.

    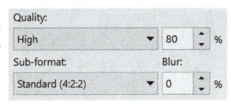

  - ✎ Please note the size information on the left below the preview image:

    JPEG | RGB Color (24-bit)
    679 KB | 99.4 seconds

- ◆ Images for the Internet should be less than 1 GB in size, especially if lots of images are used on a web page to minimize loading speeds.

  - ✎ Of course, larger images can be used with today's fast Internet. However, it would be of no use if the resolution of the photo would be higher because a usual screen can display in accordance with the size of the photo on the website.

  - ✎ In most cases, the image size has to be resized first (Image/Resample) and then the image has to be saved as jpg, whereby the degree of compression is set accordingly high.

Little Exercise:

- ➢ Save under a different name as a cpt and jpg file, with several quality levels, and see how large the files actually expanded (in Windows Explorer with the Details view).

> No objects or masks can be saved in jpg format that confirms messages in this respect. The jp2 format (jpg2000) is an extension of the jpg format, with the possibility to save additional file information and has not become generally accepted.

14.2 Use for Scanning

This function can be helpful by scanning:

If you scan with a high accuracy, you can improve the image quality with the Remove Blur effect. Only then is the image reduced to a suitable file size with the function Image/Resample.

Scanning

- ◆ Proceed step by step: Reduce the size of the image and print it out to check its quality. Do not save it until the adjustment between file size and image sharpness is optimal for your purpose.

  - ✎ For photos, it is better to save the original but documents do not need to be saved in better quality than is necessary for good printouts.

14.2.1 The Page Size - Correct Edge of the Image

During scanning, in particular, an area that is often too large is scanned into the system. These edges can be cut off:

♦ Use the cutting tool described above to crop the image.

    ✎ The frame can be corrected until the image is cropped to the size of this frame with double clicking.

♦ Or with Image/Paper Size as described on page 88 or

♦ with the Cutout Lab in the Image menu.

    ✎ First highlight an area with the marker pen, then fill it in with the paint bucket - the highlighted area can then be cut out –

    ✎ in contrast to the extensive mask tools, only "free hand" highlighting is possible with this tool.

♦ With the cutting tool you will also find Straighten and Perspective Correction. Use e.g., for straighten: move the line on a line in the picture, e.g., a slightly inclined house edge or horizon line, double-clicking on this auxiliary line rotates the picture so that this line is horizontal. Similar to the perspective correction, here, for example, a slightly trapezoidal house can be converted into a rectangular house.

    ✎ Image Slicing is intended for images in websites, here an image is not divided, as the name suggests, but divided into areas, to which various hyperlinks, for example, can then be assigned. Notice the toolbar and docking window that appears.

14.3 More Image Options

♦ Image: here you can change the color format, e.g., convert an image to grayscale or change the number of colors.

    ✎ The current color format is highlighted in light gray and cannot be selected.

Color-format

♦ Split channels to: create four images in the primary colors Cyan, Magenta, Yellow, and Black in CMYK, for example. For instance, this could be used for prepress. For CMYK, the command is also available directly under Image.

♦ Image/Rotate: If you have scanned at an inclination, you can correct the position under "Rotate/Custom" or rotate by 90° with the default settings.

    ✎ For objects, you can also find the Mirror and Rotate commands for objects that could also be rotated with the mouse.

♦ Right click on the image, then select Document Properties: Here the image data is displayed, e.g., the resolution and image size.

Chapter

15

15. Images Correction

Often the brightness is not right or the colors of a photo should be adjusted differently.

♦ Use Adjust to customize images: Brightness, Contrast, Hue, Gamma, etc.

♦ The commands to manipulate images can be found under sorted Effects: e.g., Relief Sculpture (Texture), Vignette etc.
  - unfortunately, these are not included with Essentials.

15.1 The Effect Menu

A screen that almost explains itself using the example in the menu Adjust: Brightness/Contrast/Intensity.

[Ctrl]-B

➤ For example, try Adjust/"Brightness/Contrast/Intensity" with different settings.

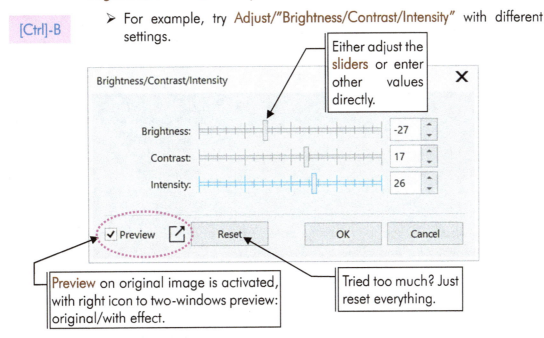

Either adjust the sliders or enter other values directly.

Preview on original image is activated, with right icon to two-windows preview: original/with effect.

Tried too much? Just reset everything.

This menu is similar to each effect. You can now explore all the effects yourself with the preview. In the following, therefore, only particularly important effects are highlighted and overview images are designed to help you get an orientation.

♦ With OK, the setting will be activated otherwise cancel or switch to another effect with the small arrow.

♦ A similar window still exists for Hue/Saturation/Lightness.

15.2 Useful information about the Effects

♦ You can repeat the last effect by pressing [Ctrl]-F or by Effects/Repeat at the top of the drop-down menu.

    ↳ There in the Effects/Repeat menu you can also select: Apply effect to all objects / selected objects / no objects.

15.3 The Menu Adjust

If you select the Menu Adjust, you can mainly change the colors. An overview:

Desaturate (makes almost a black and white image, not adjustable)	Replace Colors (pick up with a pipette, in this case, green through pink)	Chanel Mixer
		The basic colors of the color model can be set, e.g., red, green and blue for the color model RGB.

The last two effects, Hue and Tone during Adjustment, have the advantage that several preview windows facilitate the settings here.

Color Balance - Balancing image colors (here yellow fortified)	Color Hue (intensified yellow) by Hue/-Saturation/Lightness	Image Adjustment Lab...
		Lots of sliders for color temperature, tint, saturation, brightness, contrast, highlights, shadows, midtones.

♦ Gamma: allows you to adjust the color "white" from warm, bluish to cold, reddish white.

♦ At top of the menu: Auto Adjust and Auto Balance Tone automatically optimizes photos; the color values can be set manually in the Image Adjustment Lab...

    ↳ With the latter, the light, middle and dark shades (highlights, middle tones, shadows) can also be adjusted, e.g., instead of darkening everything, only the dark areas can be darkened more,

    ↳ similar to the Tone Curve described on the next page.

15.3.1 The Tone Curve

- ◆ It's a hidden gem to make images brighter or darker.

  - ↳ The whole image becomes more luminous with brightness, while the graduation curve see picture below leaves the very dark and bright colors largely unchanged because only the middle tones are brightened.

[Ctrl]-T

- ➤ Open a new photo and select: Adjust/Tone Curve.

  - ↳ Adjust manually by moving the tone curve with the mouse or use the Auto Tone Balance or load a preset. Attempt lighten, shadow and solarize (Home & Student Edition not available).

All colors from the three Channels (=colors) red, green and blue (RGB) are mixed on the screen. Therefore, you can select here to adjust only one of these colors.

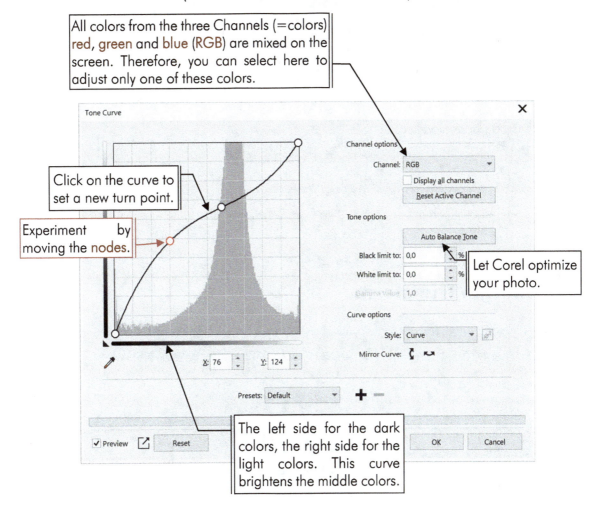

Click on the curve to set a new turn point.

Experiment by moving the nodes.

Let Corel optimize your photo.

The left side for the dark colors, the right side for the light colors. This curve brightens the middle colors.

Extreme sample:

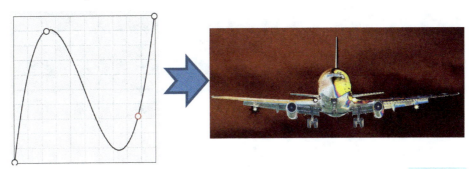

15.3.2 Other Adjustment Effects

♦ With Adjust Sample/Target Balance, colors can be replaced by other shades which can be selected for light, medium and dark colors.

♦ A very interesting feature is the Local Equalization function because oil-image-like paintings are created from some photos.

Local Equalization	Sample/Target Balance	Channel Mixer

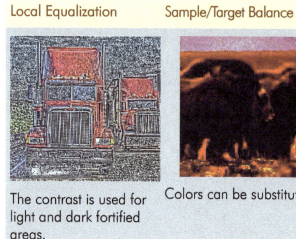

The contrast is used for light and dark fortified areas.

Colors can be substituted.

Each basic color can be adjusted.

Also, very suitable to adjust the brightness:

♦ Adjust/Gamma changes white from warm, reddish white to cold, bluish white.

15.4 Image/Transform

Following functions not by Essentials available.

DeInterlace...

Invert Colors (Black becomes white, white becomes black).

You can remove stripes for instance, when you are scanning poor quality documents (to try it out, enlarge a detail and then undo it).

Posterize... (colors are reduced)

Threshold... (to white or black grade)

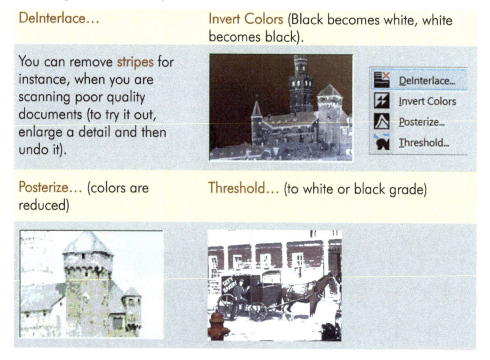

16. The Effects

These very numerous effects are shown in this tutorial with sample images because the effect can easily be seen. Unfortunately, the effects are not available with Essentials.

16.1 3D Effects

For the Boss, Glass and Bevel effects, a mask must be created beforehand. A viewing window is placed around this mask at Boss, while a tinted pane is inserted into the glass.

3D Rotate Bevel Effect Cylinder

Emboss (grey) Glass (Mask needed) Page Curl

= tinted glass

Pinch/Punch Sphere (=Fish-eye) The Boss

Zig Zag (=Waves)

To Perspective:

The Effect Perspective isn't available by Photo-Paint 2020 as 3D Effect. You can create a perspective manually by combining all objects (recommend, to save as a new photo), then masking everything, cutting and pasting - this turns the photo into an object that can be enlarged at the handles or distorted in perspective, see Chapter 4.6.1.

16.2 Art Strokes

A picture can be painted over with various print patterns. This can give the impression that it is a painted picture but a picture can also be blurred beyond recognition.

Two dogs with "Impressionist":

Please try the other options on your own. The only change is in the type and shape of the pen.

16.3 Blur

If the images are too sharp, for instance very precisely scanned, they can be softened a bit and the sharpness is lost!

In "Tune Blur" you will find a menu with preview images for the four effects Gaussian, Smooth, Directional Smooth and Soften. With Directional Smooth, edges are somewhat smoothed.

Some Blur Samples:

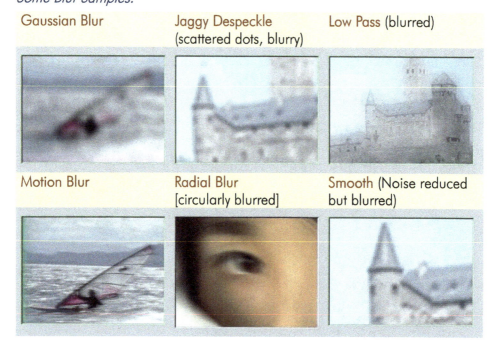

Gaussian Blur | Jaggy Despeckle (scattered dots, blurry) | Low Pass (blurred)

Motion Blur | Radial Blur [circularly blurred] | Smooth (Noise reduced but blurred)

Soften (blurry) | Zoom (radial effect, center remains sharp): | Smart Blur Details become blurred.

Bokeh is a very strong blur effect but the size of the circular or hexagonal blurring can be adjusted. Otherwise, the blur effects are very similar in effect.

16.4 Color Transform

Bit Planes (Reduce colors, select 6 or 7). | Halftone (circles with similar color). | Psychedelic with 65 (displaced change of color). | Solarize with 200 (similar to psychedelic).

♦ The tool "Red-Eye Removal" you find as an icon in the tool palette for cloning: Click on the icon and the eyes. This is even present with Essentials.

16.5 Contour

Here the contours can be emphasized in details.

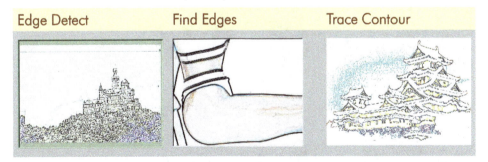

Edge Detect | Find Edges | Trace Contour

16.6 Useful Information about the Effects

♦ You can repeat the last effect by pressing [Ctrl]-F or by Effects/Repeat at the top of the drop-down menu.

↳ There in the Effects/Repeat menu you can also select: Apply effect to all objects / selected objects / no objects.

16.7 Creative

Here you will find nice effects to alienate images to a greater or lesser extent. The frame, Kid's play and weather are particularly noteworthy with the numerous adjustment options.

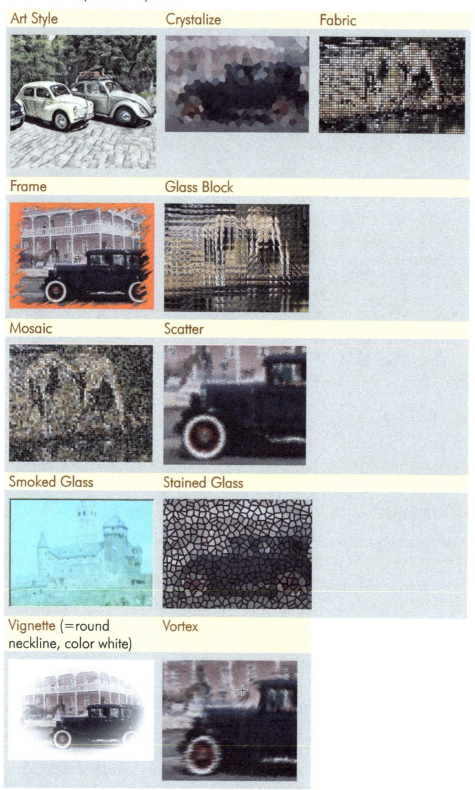

Art Style   Crystalize   Fabric

Frame   Glass Block

Mosaic   Scatter

Smoked Glass   Stained Glass

Vignette (=round neckline, color white)   Vortex

16.8 Effects/Custom

Alchemy creates structures over the image whose color and shape can be selected. Band filter eliminates the bright parts, relief map... creates relief structures and a user-defined you can select to modify the filters.

Band Pass	Bump Map...	User Defined
The bright colors are hidden. Results in beautiful night shots with approx. 50%.		

For Bump Map, patterns can be selected by "Presets:" (paving stones...) which are then placed over the image.

16.9 Distort

Blocks   Displace   Mesch Warp

Offset   Pixelate   Ripple

Shear   Swirl   Tile

Wet Paint   Whirlpool   Wind

16.10 Noise

> Noise removal = blurring? that is why image details are also destroyed! The more you remove the noise, the softer but also the blurred the image!

Corrective Action:

♦ Scan image with very high resolution, then remove noise and resize the image to fit the intended purpose (rebuild image-image).

The numerous noise -related commands overlap with those for blurring with largely the same effect.

➢ When you tune-noise, you will have all the methods and can try to remove practical effects noise:

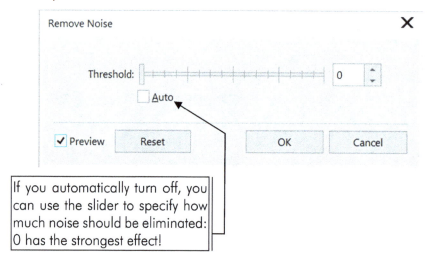

Remove Noise

Threshold: |⊢┼┼┼┼┼┼┼┼┼┼┼┼┼┼┼| 0

☐ Auto

☑ Preview   Reset   OK   Cancel

If you automatically turn off, you can use the slider to specify how much noise should be eliminated: 0 has the strongest effect!

Miscellaneous:

♦ In the case of noise, you can also remove so-called moiré patterns. These are wavy patterns that occasionally occur when scanning in areas of the same color for instance.

↳ However, these patterns are often only available on the screen, so check them with a printout before removing them.

Little Exercise:

➢ Scan an image from a daily newspaper. Enlarge this image and observe the dots it consists of.

➢ and remove as much noise as possible, then reduce the image to a sufficient accuracy.

16.11 Camera

Here both color filters and lighting effects are confused:

♦ Color filters: Colorize, Photo Filter, Sepia Toning. Note the slider for the density (=transparency) of the filter color.

♦ Diffuse, blurs the image as if with static.

♦ With Spot Filter, the image is sharp only in the center and blurry externally.

♦ Time Machine: Photos can be made to look old.

Examples:

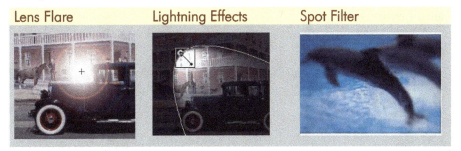

| Lens Flare | Lightning Effects | Spot Filter |

When using Lens Flare, please also note the interesting option of showing sun rays on the "Rays" tab. For clear visibility, the brightness and number usually have to be increased.

About the Lightning Effect:

Set more lamps with "+" or delete the selected lamps with "-".

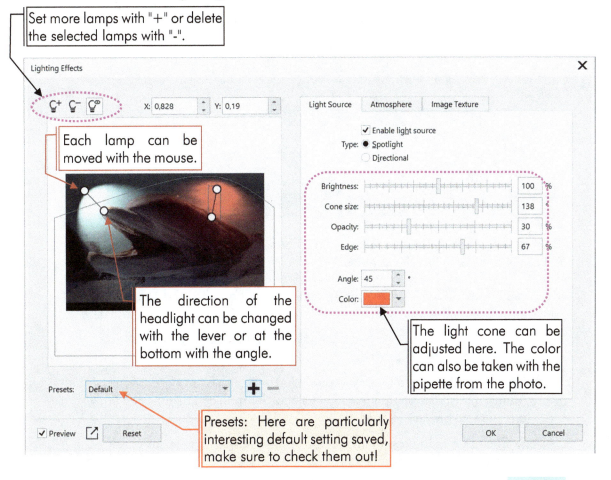

Each lamp can be moved with the mouse.

The direction of the headlight can be changed with the lever or at the bottom with the angle.

The light cone can be adjusted here. The color can also be taken with the pipette from the photo.

Presets: Here are particularly interesting default setting saved, make sure to check them out!

16.12 Sharpen

Images can only be "sharpened" to a certain extent.

> It is not possible to improve an actual blurred image, but rather it is an effect that changes the image. The more sharpened, the clearer the edges and contours will emerge.

Highly enlarged, the photo appears to be improved with optimal settings, but deterioration may have occurred in other areas or at different zoom levels.

Before you save an image sharpened, you should first save it as a copy with Save as, then compare the effect with a good printout with the original condition, because it is often the magnification that is set whether an image appears better or not.

- Sharp Image: the pixels are clearly visible.

- Blurred Image: The static is not clear, but the details, e.g., the eyes, are blurred.

In practice, it is rarely possible to achieve an improvement with these functions.

Adaptive Unsharp...	Directional Sharpen... (improves detailed images)	High Pass... (removes light colors, looks like a veil)

Sharpen...	Unsharp Mask...	

The low effect is difficult to see from the small preview images; the best way is to use the preview in the Effects menu.

The three effects Adaptive Unsharp Mask, Direction Sharpness and Unsharp Mask have almost the same effect.

Here the directional sharpness is recommended. Very fine, detailed images like this castle can be slightly improved.

- By Image/Correction/Tune Sharpen, the values for Unsharp Mask, Adaptive Unsharp, Sharpen and Directional Sharpen can be adjusted in a menu with preview images.

    ↳ Each click on a preview image applies the change, if necessary, click several times for stronger effect.

16.13 Texture

Here various patterns, e.g., a brick wall, can be placed over the picture. Because of the multiplicity herein only a selection:

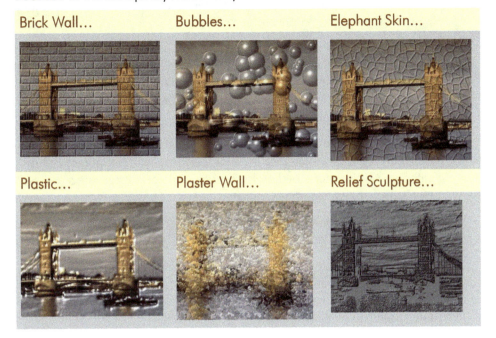

16.14 Summary

Finally, I would like to reiterate some important points:

- ♦ is a Mask in the drawing, all effects are only applied to this Mask!

  Mask

  - ✍ Therefore, only a certain image-part can be manipulated with the effect using a mask!

- ♦ Note the ability to reset all settings to their initial defaults in each Reset menu.

- ♦ Activate and deactivate the preview if the preview does not work.

16.15 Watermarks

Watermarks are used as proof of copyright, for example for images that are to be published on the Internet.

- ♦ Such a Digimark Watermark stores copyright information and contact details in a photo in such a way that it is not changed, so such a watermark is usually not visible to the naked eye and therefore usually cannot be removed.

  - ✍ Since this information is stored in the form of slight changes in the brightness of a few pixels, it would be retained even when a photo was taken.

- ♦ Of course, you would not use a photo from the Internet with a recognizable copyright without the prior permission of the rights holder, but unfortunately such protected photos have often already been copied (illegally) to other websites without a recognizable copyright,

- ↳ So before using a photo from the Internet, it would make sense to check it for watermarks, otherwise there is a risk of a paid warning, even if published in private.

- ↳ However, there is no tool to detect digimark watermarks, except for the following in the 32-bit version of Corel Photo-Paint, but you can open a photo in IrfanView (very good versatile free photo program) and in Image/Information/IPTC Data check whether an author or copyright is deposited.

- ♦ If you open a photo in Photo-Paint that has a digimark watermark, a copyright symbol will be displayed at the top of the file name, but only with the 32-bit version of Corel, because digimark watermarks are used by Corel 64bit version not supported.

  - ↳ In the 32-bit version, a photo can also be checked for such a watermark manually using the Effects/Digimark/Watermark command.

- ♦ You can register at www.digimarc.com and then request watermarks (chargeable) and integrate them into your photos. You can find more information about this on the digimark website.

Alternatives, especially for private use:

- ♦ With the knowledge you have so far, you can also create watermarks yourself, e.g., insert your name as text, convert it into a mask and then brighten this area or make it recognizable with the Boss effect.

  - ↳ Company logos or other graphics can also be stored as watermarks.

  - ↳ You can also create an object, convert it into a mask, save it to disk and use it as a "watermark stamp".

- ♦ However, there are some often free tools on the Internet such as fotor.com or "WatermarkRemover" that can remove such self-created watermarks.

  - ↳ There are two ways to protect against this, either make the watermark as unrecognizable as possible so that it is overlooked and therefore not removed, or use more sophisticated effects, e.g., instead of simply lightening the masked copyright text, replace some color pixels (replace colors).

  - ↳ The best thing you can do then is to use such a watermark removal program to check whether your self-created watermark can withstand this treatment or can be removed.

  - ↳ By the way, these programs can also be used to eliminate distracting objects such as captions from a photo.

17. Further Exercises

You have already learned the tools of the trade therefore only particularly difficult processes will be discussed next.

17.1 Painting

Note: the effects are unfortunately not available in the *Essentials* edition.

➢ Effects: Effects/3D Effects/Page Curl and Effects/Distort/Wet Paint. Start with Wet Paint, then roll up each corner.

The green is the background color of the new file.

Erasing a rectangle produces the same color for the text as in the background.

The letters were so deformed with the effect of smearing (Effect Tool with cotton swabs on brushes).

Patterns with the color eraser (different brush shapes).

The "footprints" were set with different brush shapes.

The 3D "Page Roll Up" effect has been applied several times to all corners.

Here the effect "Wet Paint" is clearly visible.

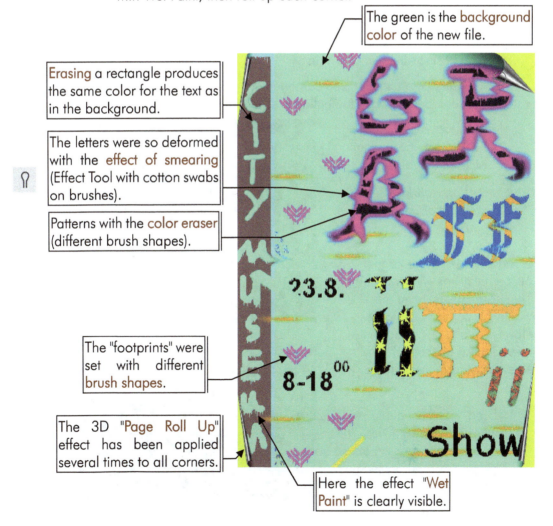

17.2 Cloning

is a function that allows you to copy in a very specific way, even from one image to another.

Open the following Images separately:

➢ Search the web for "big ben" and "aerostat" and select similar images.

➢ It is best to arrange both windows next to each other (e.g., window side by side or with the mouse) and fit them into the windows with [F4].

➢ You can start cloning with the icon shown on the left.

You will find the options for cloning in the property bar:

➢ Choose a large brush size of about 200 with a soft edge.

Start point and Cloning:

➢ Now place the starting point on top of the largest balloon.

➢ Click on the other image with the Big Ben and draw the balloon there, if possible, avoid going over the edge.

    ↳ First, trace the balloon with a large brush, then continue painting on the basket with a smaller brush.

    ↳ In the original image, you can orientate yourself so as not to get too far outside and trace the balloons.

    ↳ Left mouse button to quit and right mouse button to clone again.

Scenes that are rarely accessible in the exercise can also be designed:

Disadvantage: Errors cannot be corrected as with masks. Therefore, the freehand mask would be better in this case. However, you can correct the over-cloned brighter sky by smearing it from the surface.

➢ Drag another photo e.g., with a giraffe over this image, right click on object properties and experiment with merging.

17.3 Bitmap-Filling

In this exercise, we will place a ClipArt image before a bitmap-filling. CorelDRAW would be better suited for this but in the PHOTO-PAINT we can smear the ice with the cotton swab.

Here we go:

➢ Paint the Ice: new picture 600x1000 pixels, draw the black border lines there with the brush (switch off orbits and color variations if necessary) and fill the waffle with the color bucket.

➢ Use a large brush approx. 120 and dab the ice balls - then fill the gaps with a smaller brush or paint bucket.

The Filling and the Text:

➢ Search the Internet for "short pile carpet", copy a suitable carpet image (right mouse click on it/copy), paste it into Photo-Paint (File/New from Clipboard),

➢ mask a suitable square area (keep the [Ctrl] key pressed) with the rectangle mask, copy it, also open it as a new photo with File/New from Clipboard, combine all objects and save as a jpg photo.

➢ Now select the bitmap filling for the Paint Bucket and when editing with "Choose…" select the carpet filling you just saved, set a suitable filling tile size, e.g., 200, and use it to fill the background in our image.

✎ If the fill size is not optimal, use Undo and adjust a more appropriate value until it looks the way you want.

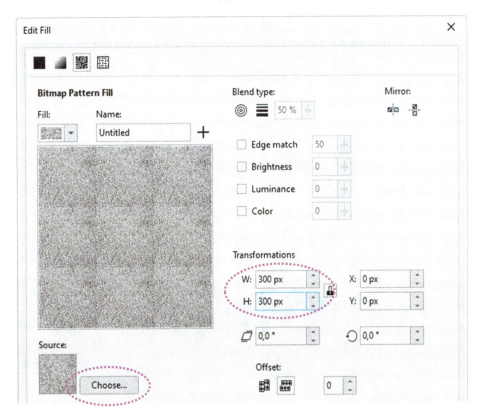

Set off text area with a rectangle:

➢ Draw a yellow rectangle below (select color and transparency in advance) as text background and add Text as shown.

➢ Add a shadow to the text, here for instance "Hard offset top right", shadow color blue and shadow gradient to 12.

Making the Ice Cream flow:

➢ In order to be able to smear the ice, it must (unfortunately) first be combined with the background, it is best to save it as a Photo-Paint cpt file beforehand so that we can access the drawn objects, then e.g., as "Ice combined" or Save "Ice cream ready" again.

➢ Lubricate downwards with cotton swabs ("effect tool").

   ✎ Try out suitable effect settings (undo, try again), e.g., smear large flat as the initial setting and increase the brush size to 200, about the same size as the ice balls.

For the frame, a rectangular mask was drawn the same size as the image, then the 3D effect boss was applied, whereby invert has to be ticked so that the effect works towards the inside.

17.4 Transparency

One more Transparency Practice (see pages 65 and 89).

> ➤ For the following exercise search the Internet for aerostat, tarpaulin or "hot-air balloon" and select similar photos.

> ➤ Open a photo with a plane from the Web as background, then another picture aerostats or paragliders, with the same orientation (landscape format), into this photo with the pressed mouse button and arrange it exactly over the existing photo.

We can change this with various transparency-effects:

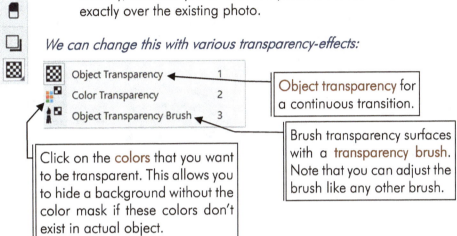

Object Transparency	1	Object transparency for a continuous transition.
Color Transparency	2	Click on the colors that you want to be transparent. This allows you to hide a background without the color mask if these colors don't exist in actual object.
Object Transparency Brush	3	Brush transparency surfaces with a transparency brush. Note that you can adjust the brush like any other brush.

Using the Object Transparency Brush:

> ➤ A brush that does not spread color, but transparency. Try it with a large brush setting, then undo it.

Color Transparency:

> ➤ Select the Color Transparency and thus hide the blue sky (click several times).

> ➤ More balloons? Copy, Paste, then Object/Turn/Horizontal and move appropriately.

17.5 Overlay Images

With the transparency tools, you can achieve excellent effects which allows us to look at this possibility again in the last exercise.

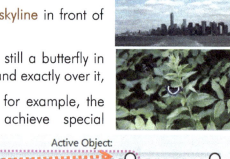

- ➢ Search, download and open a photo with a skyline in front of the sea, which serves as a background.

- ➢ Then another photo with green leaves, ideally still a butterfly in the middle, pull in the already opened picture and exactly over it,

  - ↳ right mouse button object properties and, for example, the merging effect: apply hard light to achieve special transparency and color effects.

  - ↳ If you hide the bright colors of the object a little more, then the city become more visible.

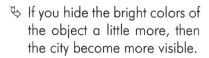

- ➢ Now draw a rectangle over it, green fill color, and set a transparency, edit the transparency and change to rectangular fountain transparency and adjust with the handles:

A fantastic new Image is created:

In contrast to transparency, object properties with the Merge function mix the colors differently so that the effects vary greatly depending on the image colors.

Of course, the normal transparency can also be combined with the merge mode, e.g., first fade out a part of the image using transparency and then the color merges.

If you have chosen a setting and want to save storage space, you can save the new image in jpg file format. However, you must combine the objects to make subsequent changes impossible.

17.6 Further Exercise Suggestions

Some more exercise suggestions for you:

♦ Scan a portion of a movie from your TV guide and cut.

  ↳ Use an ellipse mask to remove an actor's head to insert it into a program preview.

  ↳ Save the small image as a jpg file and paste it into another program.

  ↳ You can do this in CorelDRAW with import or drag the saved photo from Windows Explorer into CorelDRAW, in MS Word use insert graphics. Or simply drag the image from Windows Explorer into the open program.

You can create such a preview in CorelDRAW or in a text program so that the text can be corrected and changed at any time.

♦ Scan an old family photo and try to improve it.

  ↳ Remove static,

  ↳ Adjust brightness and contrast, possibly also the colors,

  ↳ Correct large defects (dust, scratches) with the drawing tools at high magnification,

  ↳ possibly Effects-Creative Vignette.

  ↳ Finally, try to trim it to the old state: Effects Camera Time Machine.

♦ Scan your photo and cut yourself out as an object.

  ↳ Insert yourself into one of the photos from Connect or the web and print the result on glossy paper while specifying the printer settings correctly (Glossy, highest quality).

  ↳ Trim this photo to the old state by reducing it to grayscale and adding a yellowish tint and dust and scratches. Or automatically with effects camera time machine.

♦ Review advertising brochures, posters and packaging.

  ↳ Draw up appropriate brochures.

  ↳ Advertising brochures are from graphic professionals. You can use these templates to gradually improve your design.

18. Appendix

Here are some options that are not interesting for all PHOTO-PAINT users. It's about scanning, PHOTO-PAINT settings and other functions for more accurate painting: Rulers and Auxiliary lines.

18.1 Scanning

Because scanned images often have to be reworked, please read a short manual about scanning in PHOTO-PAINT. Note: Unfortunately, the following functions are deactivated in Essentials.

- ◆ With the command File/Acquire Image....... Select source a scanner can be selected, whereby TWAIN for USB and WIA for wireless scanners connected via WLAN can be selected.

[Ctrl]-Q

- ◆ The scan program is started with File/Acquire...

  ✍ A Twain or WIA compatible scanner must be connected to your PC.

Twain

Both are standards for scanners: such scanners can be used in an image processing program that also supports the same standard. This means that you are no longer dependent on the image processing program supplied with the scanner.

18.1.1 About Scanner

If you do not have a scanner yet, some information can be found below:

- ◆ Flatbed scanners can scan an entire DIN A4 page.

  ✍ In a scan preview, the area to be scanned can be selected with a rectangular mask and the resolution can be adjusted.

  ✍ The scanner should have a physical resolution of at least 1200x600 pixels or more.

- ◆ Feeder scanners are equipped with an automatic paper feeder which is very useful if many pages of text are to be scanned.

- ◆ Slide scanners: because slides are much smaller than a photo, slide scanners have to scan with a much higher resolution (>4,800 dpi).

  ✍ With transmitted light attachments for conventional flatbed scanners, optimal results cannot usually be achieved.

Modern smartphones with a good camera can also be used as a scanner replacement within certain limits.

18.1.2 Connection types for Scanner

♦ Most devices today have a USB port. Thin cables, which can be plugged in or out while the computer is running, could be mentioned to be an advantage. With USB 2.0, sufficient speeds can also be achieved.

♦ With a network connection for direct connection to the router or WLAN, the scanner will be available to all devices in the network.

♦ Practical is the multifunctional printers of the modern day which also have a scanner integrated and can therefore also be used as a copier. In addition, 4 in 1 device also have a fax function.

18.1.3 Resolution during Scanning

Mainly, the intended use and the quality of the original determine the optimal resolution during scanning.

♦ Scan a good photo at 150, 300, 600, 900, 1200 and 1600 dpi and print it with the best quality of your printer. This allows you to ascertain which resolution results in unnecessarily large files rather than increased quality for your printer.

♦ Reference values: 75 dpi for Internet images, 300 dpi for good results and 600 dpi are sufficient for perfect prints on glossy paper with a very good inkjet printer.

> If you scan important photos and copy them to e.g., USB stick, DVD or BD, the file size hardly matters. Make backups on other media in any case!

18.2 Calibrating Colors

You should know that all devices (e.g., screen, printer, scanner...) display the colors somewhat differently, so that the printout often turns out differently than is displayed on the screen.

♦ A certain skepticism against the color display is therefore recommended, especially before correcting the colors of a photo.

♦ With Tools/Color Management (not by Essentials) you can view the default color management:

    ↳ Color management is now set up so that everything is automatic for normal users, while professional users have a variety of correction options.

    ↳ To the two index cards: Default apply general to Photo Paint while document apply to the current photo.

    ↳ With Window/Dockers/Color Proofing different color profiles can be viewed on the screen (not on Home & Student Edition).

18.3 Adjusting the Photo-Paint

In the PHOTO-PAINT everything can be adjusted with Tools/Options, e.g., automatic storage every 10 minutes (when saving). Shortcuts for commands can also be assigned during customization.

18.3.1 The Options

➢ Choose Tools/Options/Corel Photo-Paint. Especially the adjustment of the program start options can be practical:

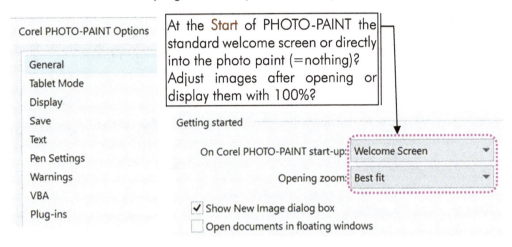

At the Start of PHOTO-PAINT the standard welcome screen or directly into the photo paint (=nothing)? Adjust images after opening or display them with 100%?

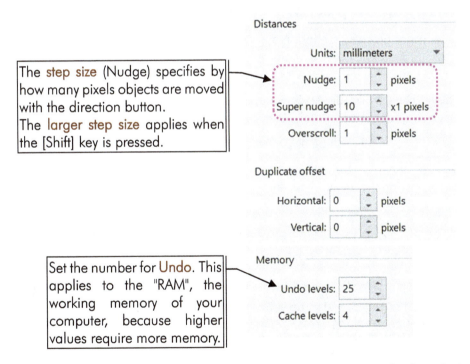

The step size (Nudge) specifies by how many pixels objects are moved with the direction button.
The larger step size applies when the [Shift] key is pressed.

Set the number for Undo. This applies to the "RAM", the working memory of your computer, because higher values require more memory.

♦ Duplicate offset: Distance between copies of selected objects created with [Ctrl]-D.

♦ When Tools/Options/Customisation (not by Essentials), you can add icons or set up shortcuts for frequently used commands.

18.3.2 Save and Undo

♦ Automatic storage can be set to Tools/Options/Corel Photo-Paint/Save.

   ↳ This can be very disturbing with large images because saving can take some time and often starts at the inappropriate moment and is therefore deactivated.

   ↳ If you enable this, be sure to set a location on another drive and still make a manual copy at least once a day on another storage device.

18.4 Printing

A detailed description can be found in the CorelDRAW book. The most important thing here is that some relevant commands have unfortunately been hidden.

♦ With File/Print, [Ctrl]-p or use the icon to open the print menu.

♦ Activate the practical print preview using the small arrow at the bottom left of the print menu.

♦ With the small gear symbol, you can set your printer.

With layout, the print size can be automatically specified,
e.g., "Fit to page" (not by Essentials).

18.5 Rulers, Grid, Zero point

These are tools for more precise painting. Not so important in PHOTO-PAINT for image processing, therefore, only a short introduction is required, a more detailed description can be found in the CorelDraw book.

In order to be able to specify the dimensions in a drawing, a zero point (0, 0) is set somewhere and counted horizontally (X-axis) and vertically (Y-axis).

♦ With the View/Rulers, this can be switched on or off.

   ↳ This setting menu can be accessed more quickly by double-clicking on the ruler or right click on the ruler.

   ↳ With *Essentials*, however, only the guide lines menu can be opened.

   ↳ If the ruler is switched on, guidelines can be drawn into the photo by holding down the mouse button.

   ↳ Double-click on a guideline opens the settings menu.

In addition to the ruler, a grid can also be set up. For example, a grid line is displayed every 5-pixel points. If the option "Align to grid" is still activated, you can also paint exactly in the Photo-Paint: View/Snap to/Grid.

♦ The grid can also be set up like this: right mouse button on the ruler, then Grid Setup. As expected, disabled in *Essentials*.

Chapter

19

19. Index

20. Overview

- ⊃ Store in tidy folders, additionally create regular backups!
- ⊃ Draw (cdr) = vector = Lines, Formulas;
- ⊃ Photo-Paint (cpt) = Pixel = Point;
- ⊃ Basic structure: Commands - Symbols, Utilities palette - Color palette - Docking window;
- ⊃ Scroll bars appear as soon as only a section of the image is displayed; rulers can be activated.

File:

- ⊃ new, open, save:
- ⊃ new from clipboard: open previously copied image as new file (also in another program);
- ⊃ Acquire image: Image scanning.
- ⊃ File/Save As: Save the drawing in another format.
  - Ten times smaller file in jpg format. However, objects must be combined and masks deleted;
- ⊃ Export for ...: Adjust images for the Internet, i.e., save them in jpg, gif or png format with higher compression. Save as png for Office.
  - Jpg is optimal for photos while gif with a maximum of 256 colors used for drawn pictures, e.g., buttons.

Deleting:

- ⊃ [Ctrl]-z for Undo;
- ⊃ Double click on the eraser to delete the whole drawing!
- ⊃ with paper paint overpainting (brush or rectangle for larger areas).

Text:

- ⊃ Text size: Select text with text tool and set font size in the property bar,
  - at the cursor points, the text size can also be changed, but, if possible, not enlarged;
- ⊃ Rotate: click again and the arrows will appear,
- ⊃ third time: arrows to distort;
- ⊃ Add this icon to the shadow:

Drawing:

- ⊃ Touch the pick tool;
- ⊃ Mask shifting, Masks,
- ⊃ Cut off image edges,
- ⊃ Zoom, Clone, Remove Red Eyes,
- ⊃ Liquid smudging and smearing, swirls, cotton swabs,
- ⊃ Text, Painting color, Image sprayer....,
- ⊃ Rectangle, Ellipse, Line,
  - with [Ctrl]-key: square, circle;
- ⊃ Eraser,
- ⊃ Shadow and Transparency,
- ⊃ Pipette to pick up colors,
- ⊃ Paint bucket for filling;

Include colors from the color palette:

- ⊃ left mouse button: Line color,
- ⊃ right mouse button: Fill color;
- ⊃ or with a pipette directly from the image;
- ⊃ Color palette for window color palettes adjustable; default: standard pallet.

Selected Effects (for Effects):

- ⊃ Creative/Vignette,
- ⊃ 3D Effects/Perspective, -Relief,
- ⊃ Distort/Wet Paint,
- ⊃ Texture/Bubbles.

Selected Shortcuts:

Undo and Copy:	
[Ctrl]-z	Undo
[Ctrl]-x, c, v	Cut, Copy and Paste
[Ctrl]-D	Duplicate selected object

- ⊃ Further shortcuts can be found in the Photo-Paint in each menu on the right side.

Zoom:

- ⊃ Zoom: Select magnifier and
  - left mouse button: Enlarge,
  - right mouse button: reduce.
  - Mouse wheel: zoom in and out.

[F4]	*Customize image.*
[F2], [F3]	Enlarging, reducing
[F9]	Full page preview (with [Esc] back)

www.ingramcontent.com/pod-product-compliance
Lightning Source LLC
LaVergne TN
LVHW081659050326
832903LV00026B/1831